OXFORD

TEACHING GUIDES

HOW TO

Teach Everybody

Strategies For Effective Differentiation

ANN CLUCAS

OXFORD

OXFORD
UNIVERSITY PRESS

Great Clarendon Street, Oxford, OX2 6DP, United Kingdom

Oxford University Press is a department of the University of Oxford.
It furthers the University's objective of excellence in research, scholarship, and
education by publishing worldwide. Oxford is a registered trade mark of Oxford
University Press in the UK and in certain other countries

British Library Cataloguing in Publication Data
Data available

978-0-19-841790-3

Kindle edition

978-0-19-841793-4

10 9 8 7 6 5 4 3 2 1

Paper used in the production of this book is a natural, recyclable product made
from wood grown in sustainable forests. The manufacturing process conforms to
the environmental regulations of the country of origin.

Printed in Great Britain by Bell and Bain Ltd., Glasgow

Links to third party websites are provided by Oxford in good faith and for
information only. Oxford disclaims any responsibility for the materials
contained in any third party website referenced in this work.

To Bob

About the author

Ann Clucas has been teaching and doing youth work for over 35 years. She has worked as a special educational needs coordinator and head of department, as well as a specialist teacher for children and teenagers with behavioural and learning needs. Alongside this, she has run youth groups and residentials, as well as bringing up four children.

Ann enjoys writing and has created resources for schools and churches, as well as the OUP online site Kerboodle. She has led training on enabling those with special needs to thrive – for schools, education centres, youth workers, and charities working with those facing challenging circumstances.

About the author

Contents

Acknowledgements

Thank you to the staff of Harbury School and Stockton School for letting me observe lessons and for sharing their experience and knowledge. I would also like to thank the staff and students at Shipston High School for their consistent kindness, help and the spirit of 'going the extra mile' over the last ten years. Alison Blake, Kate Griffiths, Phillipa Munday, Shabana Akram, David Whatson and Annikki Westbrook generously shared ideas and advice rooted in their considerable experience. I am particularly grateful to three colleagues whose example, advice and support made me a much better teacher – Jonathan Baker, Lucy Baker and Richard Harris. Thank you to Alexa and Daniel Munday, who very kindly helped create the examples of work, and to Greg Thornton, who generously gave permission to include his idea of a whole-class marking crib. I am grateful to Anthony Haynes, my editor, whose wise advice and gentle encouragement was very welcome. Lastly, loving gratitude to my husband and children who have supported and encouraged me throughout my teaching career, as well as whilst writing this book.

Introduction

This book is the one I wish I had been given to read when I started teaching several decades ago. It contains the ideas, hints and tips that I learned through trying out ideas, reading endless books, blogs and twitter feeds, going on many courses, observing my colleagues as they taught, and asking advice in the staffroom.

When I worked as a specialist teacher, advising teachers on how to support young people with all sorts of learning difficulties, I wrote hundreds of reports about children with all sorts of problems. I analysed their learning and behaviour, identified the problems that prevented them from learning, and suggested strategies to help. Later, when I was responsible for the young people with special needs and learning difficulties in my school, I read many similar reports.

I noticed that the same themes came up again and again. Similar strategies were recommended for all sorts of difficulties. I wondered whether a teacher could use these routinely, and so make learning more accessible and easier for all pupils. I began to hanker after a return to the classroom, where I could leave some of the paperwork behind and put my theories into practice. Once back in the classroom, I remembered the sheer pace and hard work of class teaching. I also realised that many of the strategies to help struggling pupils could be put in place by tweaking what I did without spending endless hours every evening preparing. If I did spend time creating resources, I decided it had to really pay off in the pupils' learning as well as by being usable time and again.

Why do the same strategies help all sorts of pupils? Difficulties such as dyslexia, dyspraxia, attention deficit hyperactivity disorder (ADHD), and autism spectrum disorder (ASD) often have difficulties in common; for example, short-term memory difficulties and slow processing speed. As every person is different, their experience of these barriers to learning also varies, but there are definitely common themes. This means that if you can change your style of teaching to accommodate problems – for example, in remembering instructions – you can help a number of pupils, not just one.

The following table illustrates how different barriers to learning may have common symptoms, and so be helped by common strategies. I could have included more difficulties and symptoms, but these examples serve to illustrate the value of the approach. I have simply filled this in with the needs of the pupils I currently teach in my mind. You can see that many difficulties have similar characteristics, so similar strategies can be used to differentiate for many learners.

Table 1: Characteristics of learning difficulties

Learning difficulty	Short-term memory difficulties	Difficulty processing spoken information	Difficulty processing text	Difficulty in managing concentration	Slow processing	Difficulty sequencing	Weak awareness of time	Anxiety
Dyslexia	✓	✓	✓	✓	✓	✓	✓	✓
Dyspraxia	✓	✓		✓	✓	✓	✓	✓
Speech and language difficulties	✓	✓			✓	✓		✓
Attention deficit hyperactivity disorder	✓	✓		✓	✓	✓	✓	✓
Autism spectrum disorder	✓	✓		✓	✓	✓	✓	✓
General learning delay	✓	✓	✓	✓	✓	✓	✓	✓

I looked at the common symptoms and then worked out what I routinely did to help overcome these difficulties. My approaches fell naturally into groups – visual strategies, supporting sensory needs, establishing routines, and so on. These then formed the chapters of this book. Although having specially created resources and extra adult support available in the classroom is wonderful, for many of us, these are often simply not available. I think that the suggestions in the book (all of which I have tested out) are doable in everyday lessons. Most importantly, they enable children and young people to learn, grow in confidence, and become independent.

I have observed teachers in all sorts of settings (and taught in a fair few myself). I have also talked with teachers who have worked in prisons, where they could be teaching prisoners who have doctorates, alongside those who are functionally illiterate. Teachers of English as an additional language can be faced with a similar breadth of ability and knowledge. Those in small schools may routinely teach children in two or more year groups together. Many teachers are used to accepting children into schools who have recently moved countries and have little or no English. On top of this, there will be young people who learn faster than others, who perhaps become quickly bored because they want to move on to the next thing.

Differentiation means providing the small steps or slightly different route to enable learners who experience difficulties of one sort or another to reach the same target as most other pupils. It also means enabling those who reach that target with ease to be stimulated to learn more, and develop the resilience they will need to tackle higher-level tasks.

I thought of many of the strategies I used as 'soft differentiation'. These strategies were often tweaks to my teaching style. There were lots of ways to create small, supporting steps to help pupils achieve, which did not involve writing dozens of different worksheets or teaching three different lessons simultaneously. I wanted to offer a variety of ways to enable pupils to understand the topic and to tackle the tasks they needed to do. I needed to guide the pupils to gradually develop the self-help strategies they needed to become more independent in their learning. I also wanted to have a life outside school. I was prepared, of course, to do preparation and marking, just not into the wee small hours.

One strategy that always helps is to know your students. To know that if George's facial expression is blank, he is processing information, and any interruption will just give him more to process. That Alex's great passion is a particular boy band, and any comment you can give linked to them will engage her positively in your lesson. Ananya, on the other hand, will always say she understands, even when she does not, because she has been bullied for asking simple questions in her previous school.

How can you use this book? I think it is a bit like a cookery book. If you are learning to cook, you might read a cookery book cover to cover to help you understand the whole idea of cooking. If you are an experienced cook and can throw together a casserole from whatever is in the fridge, you might flick through and pick out the ideas that are new to you, or the recipes you had forgotten that are easy and tasty. Similarly, if you are a new teacher, you might read this book carefully, perhaps highlighting strategies you plan to use in the next few weeks. If you are experienced, you might leaf through and pick up some ideas for a particular group, or to strengthen one particular aspect of your practice.

I hope, as you read this, you are encouraged to realise that you routinely do lots of things that help your pupils, and pick up many more ideas on what else you can do.

Chapter 1

Visual strategies

Why do visual strategies work so well? Our society now depends on visually presented information – we can all find out how to do almost anything, from wiring in a socket to applying cosmetics, by watching an online video. Our pupils are used to a world where photographs, cartoons and emojis are continually used to communicate. On top of this, many pupils with all sorts of barriers to learning have difficulty absorbing information given verbally, and benefit from a visual presentation, whether that be written, pictorial or in a diagram.

Pupils with dyslexia, dyspraxia, or speech and language difficulties may struggle to process information given verbally. Visual prompts help them understand what they have heard. Others, including those with attention deficit disorders, are easily distracted and need to be easily able to go back to the topic in hand. Those who are on the autism spectrum often need a visual link to help them move from a narrow focus to the big picture, or to support them in grasping more abstract concepts.

Learners who struggle to pick up verbal information because they have hearing difficulties or are working in a second or third language find visual strategies immensely helpful as well. Those who are anxious because the information they are presented with feels – for whatever reason – overwhelming, undefined, or impossible to reduce to a manageable size on their own can see it reduced to a package they can hold on to and consider.

What about those who can absorb and understand information very quickly? If you have clearly presented visual information for those who are taking a while to grasp it, you can afford to add in information verbally for those who need stimulating. For example, you could draw a mind map for pupils to look at and work out where a new piece of information should go. In the few moments given for this, you could then talk to a few pupils about how and where an event reported in the news that morning might fit in – thus linking in current events without overloading those who would struggle with this information.

Slide presentations, blackboards, and everything in between

Visual information includes using screens, blackboards, flipcharts and displays; giving pupils examples of what they are aiming for; and using diagrams, pictures and objects.

This strategy is so effective because you are training pupils to be more self-reliant – to expect to find the answer themselves. If they know that any adult answering a question will first ensure the pupil has looked through the information and task for themselves – whether that is a worked example of adding up, or a plan to answer an extended examination question – you are building in strategies for them to learn independently: the holy grail of any differentiation. (It also means that those off task can be directed back on task with a simple pointed finger and raised eyebrow.)

So how could a teacher present information visually without creating and printing off five different versions of a worksheet?

One answer is to use presentation software such as PowerPoint or Keynote. If you do create slides, keep the presentation simple (figure 1a). It does not need a bright, busy backdrop to try to jolly up the information. The fussier the presentation, the harder it is for students with literacy difficulties to locate the information they need (figure 1b). There are numerous slide presentations and worksheets on the Internet,[1] some of which are superbly designed. Others are so full of the school logo and learning objectives that the authors have been instructed to include that pupils who struggle to read can end up being distracted. The resource becomes the distraction. Be ruthless and remove everything that does not guide the eye to the key words, diagram or picture.

---

[1] My first port of call for resources is www.tes.com/teaching-resources. However, there are stacks of subject-specific and age-related banks of teaching resources out there and your school may subscribe to one. www.twinkl.co.uk is highly recommended, especially for younger students, and it has resources for a number of countries and curricula.

Why use simple slides?

Because they are easier to read.

Figure 1a: A simple slide

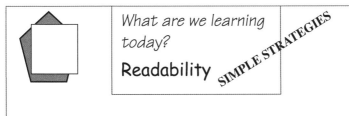

What are we learning today?

Readability   SIMPLE STRATEGIES

Why keep slides simple?

Because they are easier to read.

Learning outcomes:

> ➢ I will be able to create a simple slide.
> ➢ I will be able to explain why this is important.
> ➢ I can transfer this knowledge to creating worksheets.

Figure 1b: A complex slide: it is difficult to pick out key information

When using screens (for any format), check you have used a large font (at least 30 points), and always ensure you use strongly contrasting colours, such as white on dark blue, which can be seen easily by those with visual difficulties, including colour blindness. Avoid a red/green or green/yellow contrast as this is a common difficulty for many colour-blind people. Remember that what appears on the screen may well be dimmer and less sharp than on your computer – especially if you have an old or underpowered projector.

Avoid fancy fonts – they just make what you have slaved over harder to read, and thus less useful. There have been lots of arguments about which fonts are easiest for dyslexic learners to read. Should they be sans serif, mimic handwriting, or specially developed for improved readability? The jury is out on this. However, it seems sensible to use a font consistently so that students can get used to it, to space it well, and make it large enough.[2]

If you work in a school where the pupils have access to individual tablets or laptops, information slides and worksheets can be displayed on them as you present the task. This is often very helpful for those who struggle to keep their place when reading from a large screen. It also means that you can quickly individualise information, including translations into other languages, without much effort.

If you do use presentation slides or worksheets, make sure you save them with clear document names, in date order, in at least three locations, including one you can access at home or in a new school. This will save you hours of frustration and self-recrimination.

However, if you teach in in a school with dreadful IT reliability or in random classrooms, you may need to have other tricks up your sleeve. All you need is to display the example or instruction where it can be seen easily. Traditional resources such as flipcharts and posters still work well. Actually, these methods are so old-fashioned they have the charm of innovation nowadays. Students seem to think that anything presented using a roll of paper is enjoyable, although they are doing exactly the same work they would be doing otherwise.

The power of traditional methods was demonstrated to me by an excellent teacher I observed in a Nairobi slum school with no water, let alone electricity. She wrote the instructions and some examples on the blackboard

---

[2] www.bdadyslexia.org.uk. The British Dyslexia Association's style guide is extremely helpful and clear.

with her carefully hoarded chalk, explained them to the children, and asked them to do the work. Which they did. Beautifully. Simply presented visual information works in all sorts of ways. As long as the information is clearly displayed during the task, you are helping all those who have difficulty in perceiving and absorbing information.

What do good ones look like?

How will the pupils know what they are aiming for? What do good pieces of work look like? Learners may struggle to translate your spoken or written expectations into what they need to do to succeed. It might be that they have a very focused, single-track thought process and cannot make the leap from the instructions to what they need to do. This is a common difficulty for those on the autism spectrum. Some pupils might miss important spoken instructions or explanations because of their aural processing difficulties. Or they might be completely baffled because they cannot hear you properly. To avoid all these barriers, simply demonstrating an example of what a good version of whatever you are asking them to do looks like is extremely helpful.

Showing large groups individual pieces of work can be done with a visualiser (a mobile camera designed to show what you are doing on a screen). You can also use a tablet linked to the classroom computer, which makes the activity even more flexible, as you can move round the classroom and show the whole class work completed by pupils in that lesson. Alternatively, you could use examples of pieces of work completed by students in the past, saved digitally or as hard copies. I have also found work kept to inspire future students very consoling to me on late evenings when I am marking seemingly endless, slightly dismal pieces of work.

Some teachers make displays using such pieces of work, highlighting and labelling various sections that make the work exceptional. I think that if you spend any time on anything other than actually teaching, there has to be a payback in learning. So, if you create displays, how can they help your class learn better? If you go to this much trouble, make sure that pupils spend time looking at these. Perhaps ask them to spot where in their own work they have followed the example of the excellent work – for example, exciting adjectives or clear labels for graphs.

If you do this, it is really helpful to choose work that exemplifies a variety of standards, so that every student will see something they can aspire to. I recently taught a very mixed-ability examination class with two absolutely outstanding students who achieved 100% in their final examinations. Using their work all the time to inspire other students would have simply demotivated those who were struggling to write more than three or four lines at a time. These students needed to see the next level up for them – the one or two strategies that would help them improve their work. There was no way they could write several paragraphs in immaculate handwriting using a variety of quotations and concisely argued views. They needed to see that it was feasible to use and explain one simple quotation. (They eventually all did very well – they just needed to take small steps to get there.) It can also make those high-achieving pupils feel complacent if you always use their work as examples, if you are not careful.

Example: A simple marking comment used to guide other pupils to improve

The minute Romeo sees Juliet, he falls in love with her. He says, 'I ne'er saw true beauty until this night.' Shakespeare is showing how strongly Romeo responds to Juliet's beauty.

A good example of how to make a point, give evidence to support it, and then explain why it is important.

A variant of this strategy is to ask students to do a short task on mini whiteboards, their desk or the classroom window, using wipe-clean pens so that the writing can be removed with a damp cloth. So a maths teacher could set a problem and, once the pupils have had a go at it, they could show the class two or three different ways it had been tackled successfully by students, and then ask them to correct their own work or wipe off their work and try a second, more difficult, calculation. The joy of this is that once the class have looked at what a good solution looks like, any mistakes in their own attempt can be simply wiped away. Then the next task is to have a go in their notebooks. The differentiation has taken place by seeing what a good one looks like, correcting their own first attempt, and then transferring that understanding as they do the task 'for real'.

Just check that the ink can be easily wiped off. I speak from bitter experience.

Diagrams and pictures

Many people find it really helpful to view information in diagrammatic form. Although my art skills are appalling, I can still create Venn diagrams, draw stick people with little labels round them, or make a graph. It is always obvious from students' faces when they look at these that the penny is dropping – they understand the topic in a new and clearer way.

Why does it help to present information pictorially? Many people like to have information communicated in more than one medium. Some people put flatpack furniture together using either the written instructions or the diagrams, but others like to have both, and might even ask someone to read the instructions out loud as they tackle the job. Of course, anyone with literacy difficulties or for whom English is an additional language will find non-verbal information helpful.

A really interesting way to review a topic you have taught is to ask everyone to create their own diagram summarising what they have learned. Encourage graphs, charts and colour coded lists, as well as sketches. Sharing these different representations of the information enables students to better understand the topic without a stroke of work by the teacher.

Why get pupils to present information visually? It makes them rethink the information and work out what is important and what is not; which pieces of information link to each other; which event happens first and why. Also, if you can help learners interact with information, you are enabling them to achieve at a much higher level. For example, they actually grasp the concept of multiplication rather than simply follow the rote rules of how to do the calculation. Working out ways for pupils to embed information and then independently apply it to different subjects or circumstances is the business-class level of education.

I once asked a high-ability group of 14-year-olds to draw a diagram to explain their view of what happened after death. This was a starter task before we tackled a number of philosophies of life after death. The grumbles and questions subsided quite quickly and were replaced by the earnest breathing of teenagers hunched over their creation. I noticed there were some really interesting ideas being illustrated. It was an easy decision to drop the next activity I had planned and, instead, ask students to come in turn to draw their ideas on the board and explain them. What was wonderful was that the ones who shone at this activity were the ones who sometimes found the extended writing activities challenging. I actually got through all the information I had planned for the main section of the lesson using different students' examples. Also, the classroom rocked with laughter more than once and students talked about the lesson for months afterwards. What, to me, was even more brilliant was the gentle flowering of confidence and interest in the subject shown by the students who had previously done their work dutifully, but with little interest. I knew them better and they trusted me more. They began to be willing to have a go at higher-level activities, even if it was difficult for them. Differentiation happened because lower-attaining students accessed the learning in a way that improved their understanding and confidence.

Demonstrations

Demonstrations are better than talk. Every teacher who has ever led a lesson where experiments happen knows this. Anyone who has taught children to cook (including practicalities such as how to use a knife safely) knows this.

This is even more important when differentiating. The difference perhaps comes in the number of times one has to be willing to demonstrate. Show, and then let them have a go. Several times – and then some more. This does not take preparation, to be fair, but is difficult to organise in a big group. Sometimes you have to be canny and let the competent ones stand by the less competent ones to carry on demonstrating. Watch out, though. There will be keen types who want to help others but who think they know more than they do. If they are demonstrating how to chop vegetables, watch out for this, or have a good first aid kit ready.

Those who teach practical subjects do this routinely. An example of this is teaching a musical instrument. I taught children to play the piano many years ago. Some children would watch me demonstrate how to play a phrase of music – showing them which fingers would be most helpful to use – and could copy what I did straight away. Others needed to watch it several times. Sometimes I needed to play the same phrase very slowly alongside them so they could watch my hand as they shaped their own. Three levels of differentiation – more if you take into account breaking the task down into tiny sections and the number of times I had to repeat it. Alongside this, of course, were the comments encouraging good technique, the explanation of why this particular fingering worked (for those who could then transfer that understanding to other pieces of music) and the reminder of why this was worth it – the motivation to get them through.

When teaching a group a practical skill, watch out for those who struggle with coordination. It often helps to have some experiments partially set up (the dangerous bits at least – rubber tubes from the gas taps to the Bunsen burners securely in place) or the relevant bits of wood ready cut. It is worth saying that the ones that need differentiation in this respect, as with physical education, are not always the ones mentioned on the list or register of needs you have hopefully been issued. Just think of the stereotype of the brilliant professor who looks completely bewildered when presented with an everyday practical task.

Also watch out for those who cannot reverse the action you are demonstrating while facing them. You may therefore need to do some activities with your back to the group – for example, teaching dance steps or showing where east and west are on the compass. This became obvious when I was teaching geography recently. The group and I developed a set of moves combined with shouting out north, south, east and west to help remember this. I spent a few minutes every lesson for a week or two facing the board at the front in order to lead the class in practising this. The visual demonstration, combined with movement and shouting, really helped some of them grasp the concept accurately. They could be seen in the end-of-term exam furtively doing the moves in miniature and mouthing the words to help them answer the questions correctly.

Finally, when demonstrating, make sure you have done it in a way that is possible for left-handers to follow. I once taught a group at a youth club to crochet. All went well except for one normally exceptionally competent girl who happened to be left-handed. I later asked a crochet supremo how to do this and she replied nonchalantly that it was impossible – only a left-hander could teach a left-hander to crochet. The next week I offered to differentiate for the teenager by sourcing video clips online. Never be afraid to apologise that you did not get it right first time, and come back with plan B.

Process cards

Process cards are time-consuming to produce, but can be used with group after group if they are stored carefully. They can be used by small groups with adult help, or be used to support individuals during whole-class activities. If you have extra adult help in the classroom, pupils can create their own process cards to support their understanding.

What are process cards? They are a series of cards that break down a task into small steps (table 2). They are brilliantly useful for actions that students need to do time and again but struggle to remember. This could include cleaning up after practical activities, setting out written tasks, or how to tackle mathematics problems. They become even easier to use if you can include pictures. If you make them into a chain or concertina by taping them together (with enough tape to make a sort of hinge so they can be folded to put away), individual cards don't get lost. You can prevent them from being needed for ever as a comfort blanket by worried students by starting to cover up one or two. Once the students can remember those steps, you can gradually cover up more.

Table 2: Example of process cards for traditional method of long multiplication

1 Write the numbers carefully under each other.	**2** Multiply the top number by the '3' in the units column.	**3** Add a zero underneath the right hand column because you are multiplying the tens column.	**4** Multiply the top number by the '2' in the tens column.	**5** Now add your two answers together.
123 × 23	123 × 23 369	123 × 23 369 123 × 23 369 0	123 × 23 369 2460	123 × 23 369 2460 2829

Sorting cards

Cards are incredibly versatile and can be used in many ways. I am talking about sets of cards to match up, sort into groups, rate in importance or value, find the odd one out, and so on. If every pupil or pair has a set, you can differentiate by giving a different type of task, from very simple pairing words and definitions to more complex rating in importance. You can extend the activity by asking pupils to be ready to explain the justification for their choice.

If you have room to spread out, let students have space on the floor to find pairs of cards or to order them. It can be useful to borrow some hoops from the Physical Education (PE) department to help sort the cards into groups. (You can also use them to make large-scale Venn diagrams.)

Like process cards, these can take a little while to make. If you want to use them with a number of classes, cut them out yourself. Ones that students have cut out tend to be a little random in shape. If you are going to use cards, for goodness' sake, go the extra mile and purchase some bags and store them carefully, so that you can lift them out and use them again – either next lesson as a starter to review previous learning, or for future lessons with other classes. Seeing an evening's cutting-out work being flung into the bin because the sets are all mixed up or pupils have marked them is enough to cast a deeply gloomy pall over the rest of the day. For your own sanity, have rigid rules about carefully putting away cards.

Example of sorting cards

This example (table 3) is about the Battle of Hastings in 1066 (the Norman conquest of England when the Saxon army led by Harold was defeated by William of Normandy's troops).

You can differentiate cards by using different fonts or, even better, different colours.

Table 3: An example sheet of sorting cards

Column A	Column B
The weather – so William could sail across from France, land his large army and organise his troops while Harold was in the north of England.	William's army travelled in 700 ships.
Harold fought the battle of Stamford Bridge then marched about 200 miles south to Hastings. His army was tired when they arrived.	William was able to make sure his troops were well rested before fighting the battle.
William's army was well prepared and organised. They had crossbows and knights on horseback.	William used his archers to break up the Saxon shield wall.
Many of Harold's army were farmers.	Some of Harold's army left to go home to collect in the harvest.
William tricked Harold's army by pretending to retreat.	The Saxons were tricked and left their high position because they thought the Normans had retreated.
Harold was killed.	According to the Bayeux tapestry Harold was hit in the eye by a Norman arrow.

Suggestions to use the cards for differentiation

Here are some ideas, from simplest to most complex:

1 Give students three or more of the cards from column A to sort into the order the events happened.

2 Give students all the cards and ask them to match the cards from column A with those in column B.

3 Ask students to turn over a third of their cards at random and then ask another student to spot which pieces of information are missing.

4 Ask students to place the cards from column A in order of importance to the outcome of the battle. Ask them to justify their view.

5 Ask students to predict what might have happened if one of the events had not taken place – and then withdraw one of the cards. For example, if Harold's army had not had to march north to fight the Battle of Stamford Bridge, how might English history be different?

Objects

Object can bring lessons to life, whether they are a witch's broomstick, a Sikh Kara (bangle), or a tray of coloured cubes. Whether they are used to inspire the imagination, help understand others' worldview and lifestyle, or understand tens and digits, depends on the context.

How can you differentiate in how you use them? What changes is not the object, but the activities the students do that are linked to it. So, once you have worked out what you want the students to learn, and introduced the object, you can then give a variety of tasks that are, effectively, graded activities. Students can complete more than one if they work faster than expected. Figure 2 shows some suggestions for tasks based on objects.

A variety of activities using a Sikh Kara (bangle)

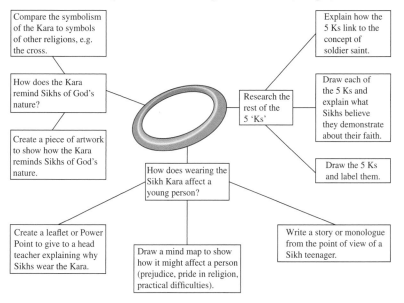

Compare the symbolism of the Kara to symbols of other religions, e.g. the cross.

Explain how the 5 Ks link to the concept of soldier saint.

How does the Kara remind Sikhs of God's nature?

Research the rest of the 5 'Ks'

Draw each of the 5 Ks and explain what Sikhs believe they demonstrate about their faith.

Create a piece of artwork to show how the Kara reminds Sikhs of God's nature.

Draw the 5 Ks and label them.

How does wearing the Sikh Kara affect a young person?

Create a leaflet or Power Point to give to a head teacher explaining why Sikhs wear the Kara.

Draw a mind map to show how it might affect a person (prejudice, pride in religion, practical difficulties).

Write a story or monologue from the point of view of a Sikh teenager.

A variety of activities using a witch's broomstick

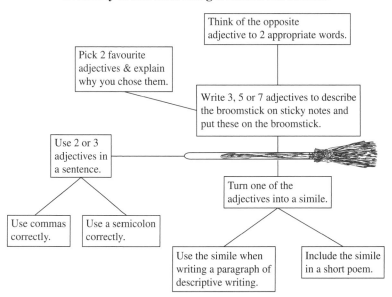

Think of the opposite adjective to 2 appropriate words.

Pick 2 favourite adjectives & explain why you chose them.

Write 3, 5 or 7 adjectives to describe the broomstick on sticky notes and put these on the broomstick.

Use 2 or 3 adjectives in a sentence.

Use commas correctly.

Use a semicolon correctly.

Turn one of the adjectives into a simile.

Use the simile when writing a paragraph of descriptive writing.

Include the simile in a short poem.

Figure 2: Example suggestions for activities based on objects

Displays

Most teachers have all sorts of visual prompts around the classroom – from the line strung across the room with key words displayed on it to multi-coloured posters of the periodic table. Very often, once these beautiful and time-consuming displays have been put up, they are not used very much. So the teacher needs to do two very obvious things to make them useful for those who need help. The first is to make sure they are at a height that the pupils can read without leaning back at dangerous angles or crouching down, and the other is to demonstrate how they can be used in the task.

I saw this demonstrated superbly by a teacher of a class of five-year-olds where the children were writing sentences independently. The teacher got up from her chair and walked over to point to the display. 'Remember to check how to spell tricky words by looking on here.' She then asked one of the children to write a sentence on the board at the front of the class. She then asked him to walk over to the display and check the spelling of one of the words. Her simple reminder and demonstration of how to use the support meant that over the next 15 minutes, all the children checked the spellings as they did their writing. The teacher noticed which children went more than once and then gave them a little more individual attention.

Visual displays of key words can also be a very effective way of enlarging students' vocabulary, both as part of their receptive vocabulary (words they understand in speech or writing, but are not necessarily confident to use themselves) and then in their speech (their productive vocabulary).

Resources: glossaries and exemplars

Glossaries

A useful resource is a glossary of words on paper that is then put in a display folder. You make a list for each topic studied in each year (you can easily draw on the glossary at the back of a good textbook). The folders can be distributed and opened to the correct page very quickly. This takes a time to set up, but is then endlessly useful and adaptable for differentiation.

When you have a resource like this, you can quickly differentiate by asking students to use one, two or three relevant words in a sentence correctly as a starter or plenary activity. You can give students two or three words and ask them to explain the link between them. The more you want to stretch students, the more random or difficult the words.

Example: Using a glossary of words linked to photosynthesis

Carbon dioxide	A gas made from one carbon and two oxygen atoms. Plants use energy from sunlight, water and carbon dioxide to produce glucose
Chlorophyll	The pigment that gives plants their green colour. Plants need it to absorb energy from sunlight
Oxygen	The gas released by plants as a product of photosynthesis
Photosynthesis	A chemical reaction that produces glucose for use by the plant

Using this selection of words from a glossary, you could ask some students what the link is between chlorophyll and leaves. To develop literacy skills, you could insist the answer was given in a complete sentence. You could ask other students to explain the link between chlorophyll, carbon dioxide and photosynthesis in complete sentences. For those who complete the first task competently you could add in something outside the glossary, such as palm oil (the growing of which has resulted in the destruction of rainforest and therefore reduced potential absorption of carbon dioxide) and ask if they can link the subjects.

Another possibility is to offer students two minutes to review the spellings of particular words, and then do a spelling test – with some pupils doing more words than others. In my experience, students never object to being let off spellings that others have to do. They also sometimes quite happily offer to have a go, especially if they feel comfortable that they are not being assessed on these spellings.

Exemplars

It is helpful to keep a selection of exemplars of how to set out and complete tasks. For example, depending on the syllabus for that term or year, you could include how to set out a formal letter, write up an experiment, or set out a long-division calculation. This means that pupils can use these for as long as needed and, when they use this knowledge for another task, they can quickly refer to what you expect them to know. I would simply add to these, topic by topic, as you teach them. You could do this by storing slideshows you have used in the lesson in a class website, or as hard copies in a central file.

Using these resources effectively depends on your knowing your students well. Who freezes at a challenge and needs gentle encouragement to have a go with easy ones at first? Who needs to consolidate knowledge? Who needs stretching and could demonstrate links between four random words? Who needs to refer back to previous learning briefly so as to do the next task confidently? Nothing helps you differentiate more effectively than knowing your students – not always easy when some teachers meet several hundred youngsters a week.

Planning written work on the wall

I first saw this technique in a training session on giving talks. The trainer used enormous sticky notes he had created. I have used the idea in lessons ever since (apologies for not being able to credit whoever taught it to me back in the mists of time). I use it for various writing tasks. First, different elements of written work are suggested by the class, written on the bits of paper and stuck to the wall. The class then discuss which order they would work best in; which should be used as an introduction, which fits best in the final paragraph, and so on.

These two stages are illustrated in figures 3a and 3b.

Figure 3a: Planning written work on a wall: stage one

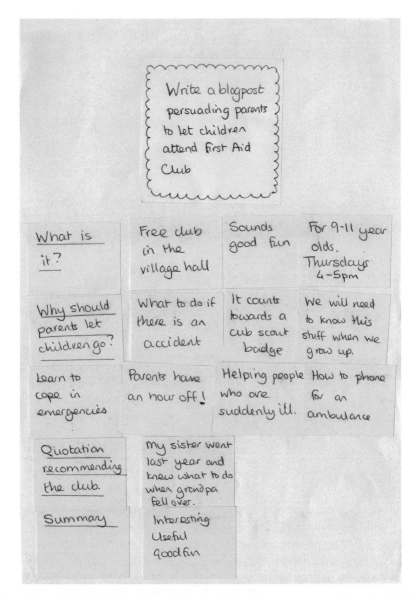

Figure 3b: Planning written work on a wall: stage two

If the different ideas are produced on a large scale, the students can then add their own comments (about messages, imagery, language, and so on) on small sticky notes and view others' comments on a silent gallery walk.

How does this support differentiation? You can ask one group to come up with more basic pieces of information and ask another to offer supporting evidence, analogies, alliteration, and so on. When you come to use the structure to support written work, you can challenge some students to turn round and not look at the display. Others can be allowed to use three or four suggestions from the display, but no more, and still others could use anything from the display that they required.

Extending activities by using visual materials

Visual activities can be quickly adapted for pupils who would complete the task easily so as to keep interest and develop their skills and knowledge. They might be asked to connect ideas – it is easy to add in one or two more obscure concepts to extend the task. They might be asked to present a philosophical idea using a mathematical concept or explain a scientific principle using a cartoon format, thus making them analyse what the most important points or issues are. Asking them to justify their views, especially in a different format, takes their learning a notch deeper.

Another suggestion for challenging students is to have a word or phrase of the week displayed, which you then challenge pupils to include in their written work. You could have a subject-specific word (with the definition and an example of it in use for those who would not know it). My phrase of the week as I type is 'rite of passage'. Some students have had to use it when writing about bar and bat mitzvahs (the rite of passage for Jewish young people as they take on the religious responsibilities of an adult). Others have been challenged to link it to the four stages of life in Hinduism. Both of these I would consider to be fairly straightforward – but then I could ask them to compare two rites of passage from religions they have studied. Or come up with a non-religious rite of passage. Or create a rite of passage with no words and symbols only. Or challenge them to create a diagram explaining the word and then show and explain it to the rest of the group.

Another idea is to present the pupils with a picture that is not immediately relevant to the word in question and challenge them to work out how it could be relevant to the topic in hand.

Some teachers have a 'wonder wall' with extension activities that can be taken when the pupils have finished their task. Or they set up 'thunks'[3] – questions designed to puzzle, such as 'Describe pacifism as a shape'. You can link these to your topic or subject. For example, if you are teaching about light, you could ask: 'If light did not exist, could there be darkness?' If this feels like a lot of work, why not arrange with a colleague to create a set each and swap them after half a term? Or you could even make the creation of the tasks and thunks an extension task for a pupil needing some challenging work.

 How to

Visual strategies

Visual strategies help people learn better. Teachers can differentiate using pictures and diagrams, demonstrations, process cards, sorting cards, objects, displays, and resource banks.

Visual activities for pupils to help learning include:

- using 'good ones' to help them think how to improve their work
- transferring learning to visual representations
- using process cards
- using sorting cards
- using displays and resource banks to check spellings, processes, facts, etc.
- planning written work on the wall.

Ways to extend learning include:

- transferring understanding to a visual format, such as a graph
- challenging students to develop their work to a higher level using 'what good ones look like'
- using sorting cards in more complex ways
- asking for connections between disparate pieces of information.

---

[3] www.thunks.co.uk.

Chapter 2

Using text and words

Difficulties in reading and writing may be due to many different reasons – there is lively debate on this. Whatever the cause, it is a massive barrier to children's learning. Each child can have a different presentation of difficulty with literacy. A child may be able to read reasonably confidently and work out unknown words by breaking down and sounding them out, but produce written work that looks like an extravagant explosion of random letters loosely grouped together. Some students will read and write reasonably accurately, but have such a limited vocabulary they do not recognise new words they come across. Others, despite regular tuition and support, struggle to make out the words they are reading as they painfully trace their finger across the line of text. Still others find that they have difficulty focusing and the lines of words slide into each other or dance a merry jig.[4]

I am not going to discuss the huge subject of how to teach children to read, but rather, how to help students overcome these barriers so as to understand the lesson content and tackle learning tasks – while reinforcing the sterling work of those who give that extra literacy support, whether that be you as class teacher or another adult.

---

[4] Visual dyslexia (Meares-Irlen syndrome): see www.bdadyslexia.org.uk/dyslexic/eyes-and-dyslexia.

Check your pupils' vision

Keep an observant eye out for those who should be wearing spectacles. A recent UK report suggested that up to a fifth of children have undiagnosed visual difficulties.[5] Added to this are the children who have been diagnosed as needing spectacles or contact lenses but who do not wear them. If you scan the class when they are looking at the board or screen, look out for those who are squinting or tilting their head. Other symptoms of difficulties include holding books very close to the eyes, closing one eye to focus, or rubbing eyes frequently. Children often use their finger to hold their place on a page, but if they continue to need to do this as they grow older, it may be a symptom of struggling to focus. One teacher of younger children I know reckons to pick up at least one pupil per class each year that needs spectacles and has not got them.

When part of my job was to assess children's reading, I always gave them a quick set of activities to check for visual problems:

- Reading simple text in different size fonts (8 and 16 points) – you are watching to see if there is any difference in fluency, whether the child moves the text with the smaller font nearer to their eyes, or whether they seem to relax when working with the larger text

- Reading text from glossy and matt paper (with text of equal difficulty but not exactly the same, as pupils will become more confident the second time of reading) – you are watching to see if they lose their place, or are more hesitant with the glossy paper, or resort to using their finger to hold their place

- Reading text of the same difficulty written in black on bright white, cream, and a very pale green or blue paper – again you are watching to see if there any differences

- Looking at typical writing on a whiteboard from different points in the classroom and discussing if there are any difficulties

- Looking at a typical slide on a screen from different points in the classroom and, again, discussing if there are particular difficulties.

Of course, these quick and informal activities in no way replace a regular check by an optician, and all children should be properly assessed on a regular basis. However, such activities can help you make a stronger case for taking the child for an appointment with an optician, and also help you teach more effectively

---

[5] www.aop.org.uk (Association of Optometrists).

in the meantime. If a pupil asks to sit at the front to see the board, this should always raise a warning flag to follow up possible visual difficulties – although, of course, they might simply want an excuse to sit next to their friend!

Helping students read

Ensure the text is readable and at the appropriate level

The first step in ensuring that the text is readable is to think about the pupils you are teaching. What levels of reading do they have? What data do you have, and what do you know about the children? Are there some who can read confidently and accurately, but often do not understand some of the words they can decode? Are there others who struggle to decode and need to read a passage a number of times to be able to absorb it? What about those who will always opt for the easier task even though they are capable of stretching themselves?

How do you know whether the text is readable or where the pupils are at in relation to the text? If students are making more than two or three mistakes per page on words that are not subject-specific, the text is probably too hard for them. One might expect problems reading 'photosynthesis' for the first time, but if the pupil is struggling with several words they should have encountered before, for example 'experiment', then the text is probably too difficult. In this case, they need simpler text. If they can read it smoothly without any difficulties but look blank when you ask them what it is about, they may be struggling with processing the information or understanding the vocabulary. In this case, they need more time to read it again or the opportunity to discuss the vocabulary (preferably with pictures to help). If they are reading it without difficulty and can explain clearly what it is about, they could cope with more difficult text or more information within the text.

So the next step is either to find a relevant piece of text or create one that fits the learners' needs. If you have a class with capabilities that vary widely, or other issues such as English as an additional language or difficulties with vision, you may need to adapt for them also, by providing word definitions or translations if possible, or ensuring the font is large enough. You may need to create a simplified version as well as making sure you have something to extend those who would quickly get bored with a simple, straightforward piece of text.

However, this can involve a lot of preparation – which is not always possible, especially if you are teaching lots of lessons every day or have a limited budget. So how do you adapt your teaching, if all you have is a textbook for the students to read and you realise that some are completely perplexed and others have already scanned ahead and are showing signs of boredom?

You may not have an ideal set of resources, but you can use a variety of strategies to help.

What can you do if the text is too complex for the student?

There are a number of ways you can help those for whom the text in front of them is too complex.

Limit the quantity

I think you need to limit what you are asking the students to tackle. Having a go at a couple of difficult sentences (with lots of encouraging nods and smiles for the words they get right) is acceptable. They could then work with a partner to discuss the rest of the passage and turn it into a list or a summary sentence so they do not miss out on the content.

Maybe you could ask them to listen to you reading the rest and try to remember three facts, or work out what happens to the hero in this part of the story, or explain why a diet full of sugar may be harmful. You ask them to focus on what you want to get across this lesson.

For those who cannot recall anything about the text they can so beautifully read, ask them to read it again and perhaps underline any bits they are not sure of, or, if it is a textbook, mark those places with sticky notes. You could ask them to jot down two things they understand and two that they are puzzled by.

Reading text two or more times

One key strategy is to teach students to read text more than once. Struggling readers very often focus so much on working out what the words are (decoding) the first time they read something, they have no idea what the text is actually about. So, routinely encouraging some youngsters to read text two or three times is very good practice. You might start by reading it aloud to them – some pupils learn better by hearing the text and concentrating on the content before they tackle the words. Maybe the whole group could take turns to read out loud. Or they could read silently and then take turns to read aloud. It may well vary from class to class.

However, whatever you do, drill into pupils who are struggling readers that a standard way to help themselves is to read something two or three times over. Only then take questions on new vocabulary (they might have grasped it for themselves from the context) and discuss the content. I reckon that, for struggling readers, generally the first read-through is to decode, the second is for content, and the third helps them put it into the context of the rest of their knowledge on the subject.

Paired or choral reading

Another way to help learners to read is to do paired reading – where the adult reads along simultaneously with the pupil. You drop out for the easy sections and join in for tricky sections so the pupil can drop out for the odd word or phrase and then join back in when they are confident in doing so. Or the pupil can read and the adult can unobtrusively just join in again when they can see tricky vocabulary looming in the next sentence.

I have also asked pupils in some lower-attaining groups to read in chorus. For example, I might read the text to them and then ask the class to read it back to me all together. It feels a little odd at first, but they quickly get used to it. Then I feel confident to ask some of the students who really struggle to read a key sentence or two out loud, knowing they have rehearsed it. It has been lovely to see confidence grow in some very diffident youngsters.

If you have a mixed-ability class, this can happen while other students read more text or do an activity like turning the content of the text into a tweet (140 characters including spaces and grammatical marks), create a glossary of the subject vocabulary in the passage, or identify the best use of an adjective in the passage.

Teaching pupils to use reading strategies

Sometimes the differentiation happens by helping pupils individually or in groups. This might be in time you have allocated in your lesson plan, or it might be just a couple of minutes' focused support during a lesson. What really helps is to not just tell the student the words they are struggling to read, but to encourage them to develop their skills in tackling unknown words.

Those who teach young children are often brilliant at routinely teaching pupils how to tackle reading difficult words. In my experience, those who teach teenagers are often unsure how to do this. Here are some simple strategies to help pupils figure out unknown words.

Read it in chunks

Put your thumb over everything but the first syllable or section of the word. When the pupil has worked that out, reveal the second syllable or section and ask them to read what they can see, and so on. Or you could divide the word up with light pencil marks. When they have read each syllable, help them to combine them smoothly. If you can think of another word that follows the same pattern, practise it so they can see that their learning has taught them to read a number of words.

> pl/ate, st/ate
>
> dr/ift, sh/ift

Sometimes you might choose to do this from the end of the word forwards, especially if the word ends with a syllable you think the pupil might know.

Teacher: What does 'tion' sound like at the end of a word?

Pupil: shun

Teacher: Good – you know the end; now let's try the next syllable between the two pencil marks.

> con/cen/tra/tion

Some formations change the sound

Remember, for example, magic 'e' (an 'e' at the end of a syllable, such as in 'rate') changes the 'a' from the 'letter sound' to the 'letter name'. So the short 'a' in rat becomes a long 'a' (or the letter name) as in 'rate'. C tends be sounded out as a soft 's' when followed by 'e', but a hard 'k' when followed by other vowels or consonants. Of course, these are not universal rules, as English has notoriously unpredictable pronunciation (for example the 'ough' in bough, bought, though, tough, etc.).

Prefixes and suffixes

Pick up if the word has a common prefix or suffix you can point out. Does the student know what this might signify? Again, you are helping learning develop rather than teaching a single word.

Use the context to help

Ask the pupil to read the whole sentence with a gap where the unknown word is. Often this will give an extra clue to add to their phonic understanding. After you have done all this, it is really helpful if you can revisit the word a little later in the lesson to reinforce what they have learned.

If the word is one of the aberrations in English that do not follow spelling rules – such as 'bury' or 'island' – just let them know and say the word.

Pre-learning

Pre-learning means using a withdrawal group or one-to-one support to enable pupils who struggle to read to learn vocabulary *before* they come across it in a whole-class lesson. It enables them to work alongside peers and develops confidence. This can be completely personalised differentiation because the support can focus on whichever part of the reading process causes problems to the pupils. If learners can work with support staff in this way, it is an excellent use of withdrawal time, because it not only develops literacy but also supports the curriculum.

If the problem is in decoding the word, a pupil's reading skills could be reinforced by breaking it down and building it back up again, maybe using foam letters. The adult could prompt them to think about patterns for plurals and how they apply to the word, or whether the word changes meaning with a prefix or suffix added.

If the issue is comprehension, then looking at diagrams or pictures and perhaps matching them up with words might be useful. Pupils can reinforce this understanding and practise their literacy by including a specific word in a whole sentence. The support staff could perhaps get them to write the word and draw a little picture to illustrate it at the back of their exercise book (figure 4). The pupil can then refer to it without adult support when doing any written tasks.

The whole activity is prompted by the teacher passing a vocabulary list for the next topic to the support staff.

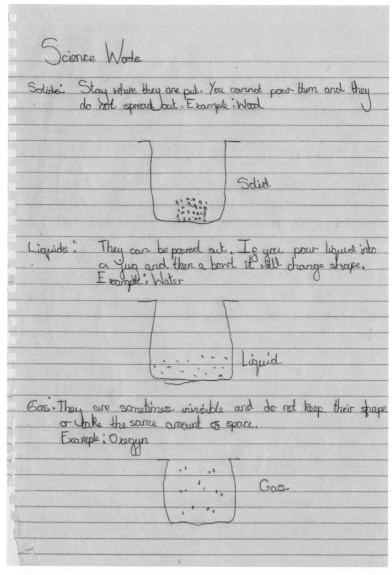

Figure 4: Vocabulary and drawings in pupil notebook

Overlearning

However, expecting some students to grasp this vocabulary because they have tackled it once in a support group and then learned about it in a lesson is both unreasonable and unlikely. Most students benefit from overlearning: going over the topic several times. Students with literacy difficulties (and, often, the short-term memory issues that go along with them) need this more than most. I find that little and often works best. So I often begin or end lessons with short activities on topic vocabulary. These can include more sophisticated and stretching activities for the more able. For example, if you wanted to quickly review the vocabulary on rivers, some pupils could be finding links between two or more words (as in Chapter 1) or explaining how a word previously learned could be linked to a related topic. Ensure they explain the meaning and spell it correctly. Others could be writing out the spelling of a key word three times or explaining its meaning to a partner. This overlearning needs to be in a continual spiral, so that the student continually loops back and covers previous topics.

Breaking down complex instructions

Sometimes students could have a reasonable go at a task, if only they understood what the task is. The complexity of the instruction leaves them struggling. I consider that making instructions tricky to understand for the sake of it is daft. However, in the real world, our students have to tackle examinations and assessments set by people who seem to relish using convoluted phrasing and many-syllabled vocabulary. This means we have a duty to prepare them for this.

Information may be given in an unhelpful order or students may be left to infer what is needed. So how can we differentiate for students so that they can eventually tackle these problems independently?

First, ask students to put all pens and pencils down and simply read the question several times. Then, get them to underline or highlight key command or instruction words. What exactly are they being asked to do?

It is important your pupils understand what is meant by any command words such as compare, contrast, analyse, and so on. If you are preparing pupils for exams, it is well worth making sure you know exactly what is required for each of these instructions for your specific context.

Next, ask them to use a different coloured pencil or pen and underline or circle the topic of the question.

Before they begin to write their answer, ask them to reread the question. This is because it is so easy to become fixated on one word or phrase and miss the point of the whole thing. I have marked more exam papers than I care to remember where the pupil has beautifully answered a completely different question from the one set. I also teach the students for my subject to reread the question at the end of each paragraph they write to ensure they are staying on track as they answer. It really helps.

You can easily create dozens of questions in the style learners can expect in an examination or assessment and go through them, getting pupils to check what exactly they have to do. If your group is able to, you can ask them to create questions (and possibly the mark schemes to go with them) for themselves.

The differentiation comes as students become able to skip parts or most of the process as they go on. Many of the 16-year-olds I teach who are going into examinations still work through some or all of this process. Others (very few) can take a quick look at a question and assess what they need to do straight away. This will be true for younger pupils as well.

Checking for understanding

This overlaps with other advice given here, but it is worth emphasising. When I asked a number of very experienced and extremely skilled teachers to name their top tip for differentiation, a huge proportion said that going to groups or individuals in the classroom and checking they understand the text (or spoken word) was one of the most important things to do.

However, going to a pupil who might be struggling and saying 'do you understand this?' is not enough. You need to ask them to explain it to you in their own words. Otherwise, you end up explaining it all in full again to the pupil who was only unsure whether to write three sentences rather than two; or leaving the pupil alone who thought they understood but missed the point entirely.

Another way to check for understanding is to do an activity that involves changing the format of the information pupils have learned. This could include placing ideas, words or events in rank order of importance or turning the text into a graph or flow diagram. This means that you can see clearly who has a good grasp and who needs more support.

One very experienced teaching friend said she had observed a brilliant newly qualified teacher who had given all the pupils in the class small slips of paper. They were instructed to write their name on it and then anything they did not understand or any questions they had during the lesson. She took these away and answered them either individually in writing or as part of the next lesson, thus providing individualised teaching. I have been experimenting with this and have found it to be a helpful strategy for students who struggle with complex tasks. Most pupils do not use the question papers. However, for the few that have, I have been able to sort out a number of misunderstandings and also enable one or two very anxious young people to feel they can write down their worries about particular pieces of work. I think this idea is particularly useful in very mixed groups or when tackling particularly tricky topics.

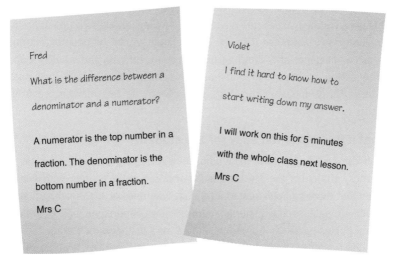

Figure 5: Examples of a questions and concerns slip

Teach vocabulary

This is a vital part of helping students understand the written word. It includes teaching general vocabulary as well as subject-specific words. At the end of a recent famine appeal presentation, one high-achieving teenager raised his hand and asked what a famine is. On checking with the class, many other students did not know the word and so were rather puzzled by what they had seen.

Improving the range of learners' vocabulary can be done in a number of ways. You could do this very easily by asking pupils to note down any words in the text they do not understand. You could then pair the pupils up to explain words to each other. Another strategy is to ask them to predict the meanings from the context and then check their findings by using dictionaries. If you teach a class regularly, you can develop these strategies as a regular part of learning.

As soon as children are old enough to use dictionaries without support, it is helpful to expect them to check for meanings independently as part of the classroom routine.

If this is to be successful, words need to be used consistently. For example, if you are teaching students to use the word 'sum' to describe the answer to adding two or more numbers ('the sum of two and four is six') then it is more helpful if you avoid using it for calculation ('you have six calculations to do,' rather than 'you have six sums').

Sequencing activities

This is where the teacher cuts the text into sections, muddles it up, and asks the students to rearrange it in the correct order. It can be done by cutting up pieces of paper and shuffling them around, or, with the whole group, using text on an interactive whiteboard. It makes students check they have understood the meaning correctly and look out for text markers, such as 'firstly' or 'however'.

What if the text is too easy for the student?

What can you do for those for whom the text in front of them is too easy? For these students, it is always good if you can provide them with extra, richer, and more complex material to read. Examples of such reading might include original source material, current news reports on linked topics, several poems by the author being studied, or a textbook for a grade higher that covers similar topics.

Helping students write

So, having ensured the students can understand what they have read, how can you help them write about it? How can you prevent the puzzled frustration of, 'I don't know how to start'?

Planning

The sensible starting point is helping with planning. The teacher could encourage pupils to write down everything they can think of that might be relevant. They could then ask them to group the information or mark it from one to three as to how relevant it is. If you have used sticky notes or index cards to record ideas, then this helps when moving suggested ideas around (see Chapter 1).

Scaffolding

A classic strategy is to produce a structure that helps sort out what to write and in what order. For example, for writing up an experiment you could have a reusable prompt sheet. Although it does require some preparation, the canny teacher will produce a version that can be used again and again. If you did a version as a slide presentation as well, it could be quickly adapted for the specific topic, activity or experiment you are working on.

Another easy way to provide a tailor-made structure for a particular topic is to provide sub-headings – and then encourage more-able students to substitute these with either an alternative structure or different wording.

Example prompt sheets

Writing up science experiments

This experiment is to find out…

I predict that…

I will use…

To carry out my experiment I will…

Table of results:

My explanation of these results is that…

Diagram of the apparatus I used:

Writing about an issue from two points of view

Some people believe…

This is because they think that…

An example of someone who takes this stand is…

However, others consider that…

They follow the rule…

Following this teaching means they…

I think…because…

A prompt sheet for younger pupils, such as the one in figure 6, can easily be adapted for different abilities by omitting some of the easier words.

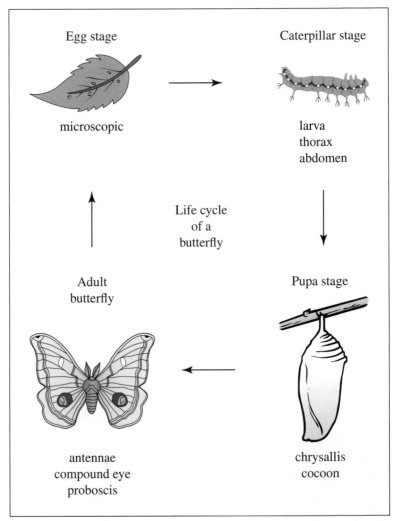

Figure 6: Example prompt sheet for younger pupils: Life cycle of a butterfly

Using questions

Training students to use what the poet Rudyard Kipling called 'six honest serving-men' – What, Why, When, How, Where and Who – means they have an instant self-checking method to think about more information to include. Often, lower-attaining students finish tasks very quickly, while higher-attaining ones need far more time to complete the piece to their satisfaction. The reason is that many pupils find it difficult to extend their writing beyond superficialities. Although teacher after teacher exhorts them to write in more detail, they do not know how to do this.

I find that asking students to create relevant questions and then to write at least two sentences to explain each answer works well. For example, a report on an earthquake could answer the following questions:

- What is an earthquake?

- Why was this earthquake so severe?

- When did the earthquake happen?

- How did the earthquake affect the roads, railways and towns?

- Where did the earthquake happen?

- Who was affected by the earthquake?

Having answered these, a pupil might then want to change the order of their sentences in a later draft, so as to make the answer flow better, and create two or three longer paragraphs.

Mnemonics

Many students find that using a mnemonic helps them structure their writing. One example is PEE – point, evidence, explain (or elaborate) – to help students structure paragraphs.

A more specific mnemonic, STEAL, could help students analyse, for example, poetry.

STEAL

Structure: What form does the poem take? Stanzas, rhyme pattern, and so on.

Theme: What is the key idea within the poem?

Evidence: Use quotations to support your answers to the first two points.

Analysis of context: Does this poem reflect other poems of the time or did it create a new format?

Language: Can you comment on assonance, alliteration, metaphor, etc.?

A good way to encourage understanding of how to use the mnemonic in practice is to analyse writing completed either by yourself, or (with less effort) by previous students, using your stash of good examples. With the mnemonic 'PEE', for example, ask the pupils to highlight the point in one colour, the evidence in another, and so on.

Cloze procedure

This is where you give students some sentences with words missing. You can give them the list of missing words (not in the correct order) or expect them to work them out for themselves. Do not give hints by including the first letter of the required word, as this means the activity degenerates into a puzzle rather than a writing activity. If you are supporting a pupil doing this activity, school your face into neutrality – otherwise they will be guessing words while watching your face to get clues as to whether they have chosen the right answer. If they do a cloze procedure, it is very important that they read it through at the end to check it makes sense (and correct if necessary) and to help them retain the information.

This sort of activity is often provided as a differentiated task in textbooks or worksheets and can be helpful if used well. It can be easily differentiated by varying the number of spaces the learners are required to complete. I think that creating these is quite time-consuming for the teacher, for what is often a short activity.

Alternative recording methods

This is where everyone in the group is working on the same topic, but they can choose different methods to show their understanding. These can include diagrams, cartoons, lists, flowcharts, and so on. This is easy differentiation because all the teacher does is set the topic and give the alternative options to the pupils. I set one group the task of explaining the structure of a traditional mosque, including all the vocabulary, such as 'minaret'. The students also had to explain how each element of the structure is used in worship. There was a wonderful response – everything from gingerbread structures to beautiful wooden creations. Little earnest notes were attached to some. 'Make sure you lift up the roof – I have labelled everything inside!' I would have been happy with a diagram, but the students really went to town. Their understanding was amply demonstrated by their comments, questions and answers when we visited a mosque several months later.

What is brilliant, when these options take off, is that the pupils spend hours and hours debating what should be included, what is important, researching on the Internet, discussing the topic with parents, and so on. It stops feeling like a task that should be dutifully completed and turns into a joyfully memorable project.

The key to this being an activity that promotes learning on the topic is to be very specific in your requirements. What facts, theories, and so on do you want the students to be able to explain? What information must be included?

Options for ways to present their work could include:

- presentations using PowerPoint, Prezi or similar software
- monologue
- speech
- scripted drama
- diagram
- model
- artwork
- cartoon strip
- film
- poster.

Figure 7 shows an example of a child's work when offered choice in how to show their understanding of a topic.

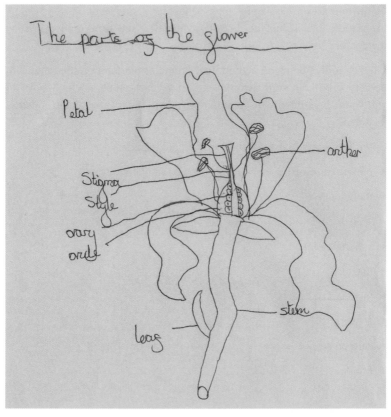

Figure 7: Example of work created from a list of options, by an eight-year-old

Consider writing using IT or a scribe

Discuss with the person responsible for supporting those with learning needs in your setting as to whether the student would be better off using a computer, voice recorder or scribe to record their work. This will probably depend on the age and stage of the pupil, and whether they will be expected to handwrite for assessments or examinations. If so, agonising as it may seem, they may need to struggle on with the handwriting because they need the practice. If they are using another format for examinations, then the more practice they can have in that format, the better.

Some pupils find typing very helpful, because they can simply write down thoughts as they occur to them and then reformat them into the order they want and improve the vocabulary and structure of the piece of work. If they are to type their work routinely, then pupils could learn to touch type, if they are not already fluent.[6]

Many students are familiar with speech recognition software used to find information or give instructions to computers. The dictation packages available for writing text are increasingly sophisticated and can be a very useful tool, especially for those who find handwriting and typing difficult.[7]

However, dictating more than a simple instruction involves a sequence of skills that need to practised.

The person needs to decide what to say and then say it aloud phrase by phrase (while retaining the structure of the whole sentence, or even paragraph). At the end of this, the script needs to be checked for mistakes. This can be supported by the read-out-loud facility.

The key to using dictation packages productively is to use them regularly, especially as the computer program can learn to interpret accents and an individual's speech patterns.

Using the correct pen to help handwriting

Some schools, especially those for younger children, have strict policies about the writing implements used. Special certificates are often given out to mark a child's move from pencil to pen, and only certain sorts of pen are used. Other schools let the pupils use whichever pen they choose. The problem comes when the pen chosen by the school in the former case does not suit the child and the pen chosen by the child in the

---

[6] www.bbc.co.uk has a helpful resource called Dance Mat Typing.
[7] Dragon NaturallySpeaking is a good program for this.

latter case is a scratchy old biro. The poorer a student's handwriting, the weaker their fine motor skills, the more important it is that they have a pen that suits them.

A really simple resource for any teacher is a pencil case full of various types of pens and pencils (including different shapes, grips and fibre tip or gel), additional grips, and a ruler with a raised handle.[8] Students can then experiment with different types of writing implements to find whichever one suits them best. Alternatively, you could encourage parents to take children to a stationer where they can try out a variety of pens to see which suits them.

Those that prefer to write in pencil often like a pen with a slight drag to it such as a fibre-tipped pen. If they like a gel pen, it needs to be of reasonable quality so that the flow is even. Pens that are very narrow often cause aching muscles from an overly tense grip. Some of my pupils, otherwise worldly, sophisticated types, love using the rubbery pencil grips often used by those learning to write. They find they can write for much longer without cramped muscles. It seems ridiculous that we pay out a fortune for new textbooks or fancy IT kit when students are using pens that are inappropriate for their needs.

Helping the gifted and talented to develop their writing

You can differentiate for these students by offering them a more complex task. This could mean that when they have written up their science experiment, they then compare it with another. Or, if they are explaining the causes of a war in history, ask them to demonstrate how a source could be interpreted in two ways. Another option is to challenge them to include more complex vocabulary.

An alternative approach is to ask students to pare down their writing. Rather than making it more and more complex, you create artificial constraints such as an exact word count or a limit on the number of words in each sentence. This is useful for those able students whose language seems to become ever more elaborate but who sometimes struggle to communicate clearly.

---

[8] www.thedyslexiashop.co.uk is a good source for all sorts of writing resources.

How to

Using text and words

To help students overcome barriers in reading:

- Check your pupils' vision.

- Ensure the text is readable and at an appropriate level for the pupil.

- If the text is too complex for the student: limit the quantity to be read; read two or more times; use paired or choral reading; teach pupils to use independent reading strategies; organise pre-learning; build overlearning into your lessons.

- Break down complex instructions.

- Check for understanding.

- Teach vocabulary.

- Give sequencing activities.

- Extend reading tasks for gifted and talented by offering a variety of extra reading at a higher level.

Help students overcome barriers in writing by:

- helping them plan

- helping them structure by scaffolding, creating questions to answer in their work, and using mnemonics

- using cloze procedure tasks

- students' choosing alternative recording methods

- using IT or a scribe

- using a helpful pen.

Extend writing tasks for gifted and talented by:

- requiring more, or

- setting artificial constraints.

Chapter 3

Changing the task

We want all children to achieve. For this to happen, some will need tasks and class activities presented differently or changed to support or extend their learning.

Students who are anxious (including those with additional difficulties and barriers to learning) will thrive in a classroom where they feel safe and able to tackle the task without feeling they will look foolish. For example, asking a colour-blind student to shade in a map of mountains according to height using graduated colours is probably asking them to do something they cannot do. Graduated browns and greens, or blues, purples and greys may be impossible to distinguish. This will be obvious to their neighbours as soon as they attempt it and they will become vulnerable to teasing. They may need to use stripes or dots in their map to achieve the same task. Similarly, telling a dyslexic student to skim and scan a document and make succinct notes may well be completely unhelpful to their learning as they will struggle with the process and mostly fail to absorb the content. Instead, asking them to read the headings within the text and highlight specific words, then write one phrase to sum up each section or paragraph, breaks down the task for them.

The tasks set should help pupils engage with the topic, develop their knowledge, and enable them to practise the skills needed for the subject. Breaking down the task so that it is easily grasped by those who struggle to work out what is being asked of them means that once it is complete, you can guide the student to see the big picture – how this learning fits into the grand scheme of things. Other students might need the task adapting so they can use props to help understand and internalise the concept, or to enable them to do less writing, or record in a different way.

In order for all pupils to access what they need to learn, the teacher needs to be crystal clear what the aim of the lesson is. Is it to improve a skill, for example writing a recipe clearly, or is it to learn new information and be able to explain it and link it to the main subject? Once the teacher is clear on this, breaking down the task or setting activities that genuinely extend rather than fill time is often relatively easy and the teacher can habitually make the learning accessible to all.

However, in order to clarify what exactly the students need next, the teacher needs to have a range of easy ways to formatively assess the class. This simply means the teacher's ways of working out what the pupils know and can accomplish. Again, these actions can become routine and take very little time and effort.

Formative assessment

Formative assessment by walking around

There is no better formative assessment than listening to students and looking at their work. It sounds obvious, but it is part of the routine of teaching that effective teachers use all the time. You can develop this further by using your knowledge of students and then deciding who to go and see first. This might be a group who habitually struggle to settle. You can check they know exactly what they need to do by asking them to explain the task back to you.

Some schools have a policy of teachers walking over and talking briefly with any underachieving students before circulating the rest of the class. It can also help to have a brief word with those who are likely to complete the task quickly and accurately – direct them to the extension activity so they do not need to interrupt you later. You might choose to start at a different point in the classroom each lesson to ensure that all pupils get time with the teacher. Whatever you do, think about why you do it rather than fall into the habit of going to the most disruptive, or the low attainers, or those nearest the back every lesson, without realising you never get to the quiet group who sit in the middle and just get on with whatever they are told to do.

Some teachers may choose to sit with a group for 20 or 30 minutes and work with them. This often works well if there are support staff who can keep the other pupils on track. It can take some time to train the students to work independently, but it is well worth it.

Formative assessment by reading work

A quick read of a class's work will often clarify exactly what needs to happen in the next lesson. Useful as marking work can be, it is more important to have a quick check of what has been done and find out whether you can move on or need to go over a topic that has not been understood – even if it is for only a small group while the other students tackle something else. This is true personalised differentiation.

It might be worth investing in an ink stamp or something similar to indicate the books you have quickly read so that the students know you have perused their work.

A recent example of this is when I flicked through the work of a class of 11-and-12-year-olds and realised that quite a few had mixed up the Jewish festival of Passover with the Hindu worship ceremony, puja. It looked like they understood what happened at both events, but had mixed up the names – an easy muddle to correct the next lesson. However, had I not checked their work, the pupils would have become very confused during the next lesson and the mistake would have become embedded in their memory.

Formative assessment by quizzes

These are an easy way to check knowledge. There are now many online versions of quizzes or questions for the end of a lesson, and they can be very useful.[9] However, they can be a source of anxiety and counterproductive if it is not made clear that they are not part of your summative assessment (i.e. marked and noted down by the teacher as part of the record of progress made by a pupil). If quizzes are self-marked or swapped with a partner, the mark could be recorded in the back of exercise books – when the books are handed in you could glance over them. If having looked at them, you think the topic needs readdressing in some way, you could use the same quiz next lesson and, hopefully, encourage the students to celebrate their now-improved mark.

Example of a multiple-choice quiz question for checking knowledge

What is the name of a bend in a river?

a) Meander (correct answer)

b) Mean

c) Shore

d) Liquid

You might include words similar in meaning to the answer – but make sure that there are no real difficulties in working it out.

If you write a multiple-choice question carefully, you can also check for understanding. The distractors need to be common misconceptions and mistakes. You can ask students to elaborate and explain as you discuss the answer.

Example of multiple-choice question for checking understanding

Which of the following helps form a meander?

a) The water is fast flowing.

b) The river is in its middle course.

c) Moving water erodes the inner banks.

d) Moving water erodes the outer banks (correct answer).

---

[9] www.whiteboardblog.co.uk is one website that gives a selection of quiz formats.

Here, a student would need to think about the way meanders are formed. They may, of course, make a lucky guess, but this question tests understanding rather than simply knowledge.

Formative assessment by students reporting back on their own understanding

This can be very easily done by asking students to do a thumbs up, down, or midway signal depending on their level of confidence, or a 1–5 rating using the fingers of one hand. If you think they would be more honest in their self-assessment if other pupils were not watching, ask the whole class to close their eyes so they can feel anonymous.

Some student planners have a page that is red on one side and green on the other. Asking students to have their planners open at this page and use the red page to signal help needed and the green page to signal they understand and can do the task gives you a clear sense of the class's progress by just glancing around the room. This strategy could easily be replicated with cards that are red on one side and green on the other.

An increasingly popular version of self-assessment is asking students to complete an 'exit slip' at the end of a lesson – often with emojis to circle or questions to answer. Again, these are often used to record levels of confidence in understanding of a topic. The problem with some of these strategies is that the student may feel an entirely misplaced confidence or be embarrassed to say they think they have succeeded because it feels like boasting. So the more specific the rating activity, the more useful the activity as formative assessment. You could make the sign-off to the lesson a question about the topic that has to be answered on the exit slip, which would give you an accurate feel for the level of understanding.

Example of an exit slip

Name:
Three facts I have learned:
A question I have is:
Answer to 'exit slip' question:

Formative assessment activity within the lesson

Activities with mini whiteboards and pens work well for this. You could, for example, ask the class to write down the square root of 16 or three characteristics shared by mammals – whatever is the topic of the moment. They then hold up their whiteboards for the teacher to see. This is a very helpful strategy because you can see instantly who has the correct answer.

Alternatively, asking students to write down answers or suggestions on sticky notes and putting them on the whiteboard can be useful, because once they have brought them up to the board you can feed back a wide variety of answers very quickly to the whole group, thus assessing what they know or understand as you share a variety of ideas.

Formative assessment by questioning

In order to do formative assessment in a question-and-answer session, the teacher needs to move away from the 'hands-up' method, because only a small proportion of the students are likely to routinely offer to answer questions. Those who are unsure of the topic, find large group activities difficult, are disaffected, or who have poor concentration are unlikely to raise their hands. However, the opposite strategy – with no hands up and the teacher either randomly picking students via a name-chooser program[10] or selecting from a jar of lolly sticks the students have written their names on – also brings difficulties. It can raise anxiety for students who do not realise the teacher will adapt the question to suit them if their name is called. This can be overcome by the teacher having a quiet word with such students to reassure them and perhaps suggest a private signal if they are feeling particularly worried or vulnerable.

If a pupil gives an incorrect answer, reply with praise for having a go. Explain that we all learn from getting it wrong and by being brave enough to try. They have helped everyone learn and we can go on to learning it correctly. I sometimes feel that I come out with this line too often, but it really does seem to make a difference as to whether students have the confidence to attempt answers. Depending on the class, it sometimes works to pause and ask anyone else who had a similar incorrect answer to raise their hands. (You have to be sure that at least one other person will be honest and confident enough to do this.) You can then boost the student by praising them for helping all those who were similarly confused.

---

[10]Such as www.classtools.net.

It is helpful to make it clear whether you are asking a question with one correct answer ('What is the name of the capital of France?') or a genuinely open one ('Who do you think was the most wicked character in Hamlet?') In the case of an open question, students should then be asked for their reasons. 'Dunno' is not acceptable.

The teacher can target questions for specific students, thus checking their knowledge and understanding. The questions can range from very simple choices between an incorrect and correct answer (giving confidence to the worried student) to sophisticated comparisons or predictions. It is worth having a series of question starters for your subject or suitable for your pupils' ages at the back of your planning folder so you can develop the skill of asking questions without too much preparation – if any. It will be one of the most useful tools you have in teaching effectively. Using a taxonomy of questions gives you information about how much your students know, while developing their understanding. There are many examples of these on the Internet, Bloom's taxonomy being the most famous. Here are some ideas:

Question starters

Subject knowledge – these questions are asking for factual pieces of information. They often begin with who?, what?, where?, when? or how many?

Understanding – these questions are asking students to use one or more facts and link them together in some way. They often begin with how?, explain, describe, or what caused?

Using knowledge and understanding – these questions are often in two parts. They ask the student to analyse the topic (identify and evaluate the constituent elements). For example:

- 'Which is the most important? Why?'

- 'Is there anything illogical in this? What evidence do you have for this?'

- 'If you were to apply this theory to X, what outcome would you predict?'

Links to other subjects (the bigger picture)

This is where the student is not analysing a topic but synthesising – that is, connecting their knowledge to a larger picture. So, for example, a student working on the French revolution may be asked to compare the events in that period in America, France and England and explain how they are linked together. If they are able to link in how these events might have affected Mary Wollstonecraft as she wrote about women's rights or William Blake as he worked on his poem 'Jerusalem', they are beginning to have a rich understanding of history and literature. Similarly, a student working on different religious views on abortion who can explain how a new diagnostic tool for Down's syndrome might affect the actions of different groups within Christianity has moved a long way from recounting facts to having a deep understanding of how beliefs change lifestyle.

Allow thinking time

Getting the timing right when you ask questions is really important. Many learners need time to process and cannot come up with an instant answer. You can easily overcome this by asking the question and then, if they look at all hesitant, letting them know you will come back to them for the answer in a few moments so they can think about it. It is often a good idea to ask the question and announce 20 or 30 seconds' silence for everyone to think – with the understanding that you might choose anyone to answer. If, after this, someone still comes up with a blank – either they just have not bothered to think, or a worried or frozen expression indicates they are genuinely struggling – you can suggest they listen to others' answers and you will return to them later. They can repeat an answer they hear from someone else if need be. This thinking time need not be wasted for higher achievers – you simply ask anyone who is likely to have an answer ready quickly to think of two more examples, or be ready to demonstrate the calculation to the class, or think of the opposite to the concept you are discussing.

Another way to overcome the difficulty is to get everyone to write down an answer on their mini whiteboard so they have something to read out. Or you could ask everyone to think and then turn to their neighbour and share their thoughts and between them come up with a complete sentence to offer to the class.

Ways to change the task

Graded success criteria

When teachers have a particularly broad range of ability in a class, they often turn to this strategy. For example, a teacher with a class that includes four-year-olds alongside nearly-six-year-olds is teaching some children who are almost half as old again as the youngest ones. Differentiation is absolutely vital, especially if you add in the possibility of learning difficulties – many maybe as yet undiagnosed.

The key is to work out what would be the next step for each pupil or group and record that – maybe in their books or by a code in a mark book. Once the teacher has thought about the focus of the lesson and completed a simple record of the different criteria and therefore the focus of teaching, it is relatively simple to differentiate very effectively by grouping the pupils, providing different resources, or simply by giving different tasks (tables 4a and 4b).

Table 4a: Example of graded success criteria: younger pupils

Code	Activity	Teaching focus
A	Write the names of three animals and draw them.	Correct formation of letter 'a'
B	Write a simple sentence about the appearance of one animal.	Use a capital letter and full stop.
C	Write three sentences about the appearance of one animal, using adjectives.	Check use of capital letters and full stops. Use of adjectives.
D	Write a paragraph about the appearance of one animal, using adjectives and a simple connective.	Check use of capital letters and full stops. Use of adjectives and connectives.

Table 4b: Example of graded success criteria: older pupils

Code	Activity	Teaching focus
A	Write a short paragraph to explain how the author has used similes and metaphors, using one example of each.	Accurate identification of similes and metaphors.
B	Write an extended paragraph to explain how the author has used similes and metaphors, using several examples of each.	Demonstrate how similes and metaphors help the reader understand the text in a deeper way.
C	Identify and explain examples of similes, metaphors, and pathetic fallacy in a well-organised extended paragraph.	Accurate identification of pathetic fallacy and demonstrate how all three literary strategies help the reader understand the text in a deeper way.

Another way to do this is to do an opening activity with the whole class to compile a set of relevant success criteria. They can then copy this into their exercise book and highlight one they are going to focus on. You can then circulate the class and highlight another criterion in a different colour, either for students that need to aim higher or to make sure they have achieved one of the more basic aims. You can also add a very specific one for particular students.

Example of the success criteria suggested by a class

Success criteria for an examination answer

- Use subject-specific vocabulary.

- Use two sources and explain how reliable they are and why.

- Use three sources and explain how reliable they are and why.

- Explain the context of the issue discussed.

- Include two points of view.

- Use well-constructed paragraphs.

- Summarise the arguments in a final paragraph.

Adapt speed of tackling the task

This is an easy way to differentiate. Simply offer more time to do the task or make the task shorter. Alternatively, you can challenge those who might be coasting by giving them a shorter time to complete the task.

One group who benefit from this adaption is children who speak English as an additional language and who need time to process academic material. Although some seem to become fluent in English incredibly quickly, it is social language in which they have become fluent. If they are dealing with more sophisticated concepts, they may well be translating them into their first language in their head in order to consider them. Once they have got the answer or concept ready to explain, they then re-translate back into English. This obviously takes time to accomplish.

However, if you are going to use this strategy, you need to be aware that some people have real difficulty understanding time. Learning about time does not only cover being able to read a clock face (although reading both digital and analogue clocks is a fairly sophisticated skill that some never completely master). Sometimes those with dyscalculia – difficulty understanding the concept of numbers and therefore using them – and dyslexia, as well as other allied difficulties, struggle to understand what, for example, ten minutes feels like. This means that if you are to adapt the time for a task, it might be helpful to actually show learners how long they have got by pointing to the correct place on a clock face or by using a timer of some sort, especially for young children.[11] If you are suggesting the task is continued over a number of days, this may need writing down for the pupil so it can be ticked off as session 1, session 2, and so on.

[11] A selection of timers can be found at www.thedyslexiashop.co.uk.

Many learners need to learn how to use extra time given for a task. You could suggest that they reread a text once or twice more. Perhaps they need to write down their thoughts on a mini whiteboard and then put them into a plan in their book before they write. It could be useful to look at a worked calculation again and talk themselves through how to do it out loud before they start working on one independently. When you train students to do this, you are training them to become independent workers who use self-help strategies and succeed with little intervention.

Tasks that develop in difficulty

This can work well, especially if you do not expect all pupils to start at the beginning or work through to the end. One teacher who had worked in the difficult environment of a school for young prisoners – some of whom had hardly attended school and were barely literate, while others were exceptionally high achievers – used for her guidelines three scaffolded activities, three open-ended questions, and an extension task that included writing at length. This gave each student something meaningful to do and gave her time to give to each group in turn, as the class were meaningfully occupied. Obviously, if you were teaching mathematics, your extension task would be a little different – possibly a word problem that uses the skills practised or a complex diagram illustrating the understanding of the geometry learned.

Check the tasks you have chosen reflect what you want students to learn or practise, rather than simply occupy them. Figure 8 shows an example of such a lesson plan.

The downside of this strategy is that some pupils will only ever tackle the first group of questions, and so do not get to explore the higher-level tasks. For those who have difficulty in specific areas of learning (such as reading or handwriting), but who have good abilities in understanding the task, this is very frustrating. The student who struggles to record but who can give a lively and accurate description of the topic in hand would end up always answering basic questions. The answer is to be flexible in what you ask each learner to do. So, as you go round the class, you could put dots by the specific questions or activities you expect such a student to tackle. Also, you could add in an activity that might show their understanding in a different way, for example, drawing a diagram.

Using props

The word 'props' often calls to mind the manipulatives used in mathematics teaching. However, I have broadened the concept to other subjects and age groups. The props I refer to include a range of visual aids, not just items that need to be picked up and moved around by the student.

Cover lesson plan

Date 14 December 2017	Class 4c	Room Lab1
Lesson 3	Teacher AC	Number of students 25

Context
2nd lesson on classifying materials following practical lesson exploring and categorising a variety of materials

Learning objective
Describe differences between gases/liquids/solids
Describe the behaviour of particles in gases, liquids, solids

Starter
Students to look back at their experiment reports from last lesson and identify a verb, an adjective and an adverb.

Structured activities
    1. Read pp.11–12 in textbook and answer questions 1–5
    2. Read p.13 in textbook and answer question 6
    3. Read p.51 in red textbook and answer problem 4
Group 1 to do activity 1, group 2 to do activities 1 and 2, group 3 to do activities 1 and 3

Open-ended activities
    1. Write a list of 3 gases, 3 liquids and 3 solids
    2. Create a mind map of the different qualities for gases, liquids and solids
    3. Create a list of substances that change, eg ice/water/steam.
Students can choose which of these activities they do – they can do more than one of them if they work quickly.

Extension activity
Are these items gases, liquids or solids: fire; eggs; jelly? Explain the reason for your answers.

Plenary 'Gas, liquid, solid' game – we played it last lesson. This time ask the students to explain the rules to you. (When you call out 'solid' they all bunch together; 'gas' - they all move around, and 'liquid' - they are near to each other.)

Please see classroom plan for groupings and information on additional needs.

Figure 8: Cover lesson plan with three structured activities, three open-ended activities, and an extension activity

One very quick way to change the difficulty of the task is to add in support materials. These can include anything from blocks or Numicon[12] to help those working on arithmetic to copies of the text of *Romeo and Juliet*.

Some props help learners visualise and then internalise abstract concepts (for example, three plus three always equals six). Examples of these types of props are cubes, shapes, number lines and number squares. When learning to read and write, foam letters – both single and blends such as 'ng' – can be extremely helpful, as the children are encouraged to go over the shapes with their finger and say the sound out loud before they use them to create words or check spellings.

Some young people need props to help for a long time. Many children who are used to having these routinely available to help them find they have disappeared when they move to a secondary school. If props are to be useful to any group, they need to be a visible and unremarkable resource in classrooms – not stashed in the back of the stockroom and hauled out when a pupil has repeatedly failed at a task.

Props also help those who cannot hold one piece of information in their head while they work on another. It can be difficult to focus on writing good sentences that answer a question on Henry VIII (the well-known sixteenth-century English king) while also remembering his family tree. Even if it is in the textbook a few pages back – flipping back and forth to help recall the information can interrupt concentration. Simply having two copies available, each open at the relevant page, can help. An alternative to this is to have one set of information available on the classroom screen.

Props also benefit those who are adding in yet another skill because they are working in their second or third language. Props enable higher-level thinking because the focus of the task is not diluted by trying to remember factual information.

They can be used in many subjects. A science experiment ready set up and on display would help a student trying to write it up at a later date. Students working on history might find a timeline helpful. Those learning to play keyboard could use a picture of a piano keyboard with the names of the notes identified on staves just above the keys. These props are in many textbooks, or easily available on the Internet, or would often only take a few minutes to create. The time is well spent, as although some students will be able to look at them and then move on, others need them in front of them as they work.

---

[12] Numicon is a brilliant method of teaching numbers. It is marketed through www. global.oup.com.

Using groups

Group work is a strategy that provokes very mixed views in teachers. Many feel it promotes higher-level learning for all; that it can help develop interpersonal skills needed throughout life, as well as encouraging critical thinking and problem-solving strategies. Others note that in many groups one or two students do the work while others sit back. Shy students may struggle to join in. Sometimes all that happens is a pooling of ignorance rather than a deep and rich educational experience.

If asked, most students say they learn best working in groups. My experience for many years was the complete opposite. The pupils enjoyed the lessons where they worked in groups, but their learning was consistently poorer. Often, the work produced by a whole group was inferior to the work they would all have produced individually if they had worked in that way. So I have learned the hard way how to use groups to change the nature of the task and enhance learning.

Thinking about what you hope the groups will achieve and who will be in each group is really important. Almost every time I have let pupils choose their own groups for an extended activity or task, I have regretted it. If you include group work regularly, you may want to adapt your seating plan accordingly. The groups need to be carefully chosen for your purposes. What size are they and what do you want them to achieve? Pairs of students to quickly come up with three suggestions, or groups of six to create a dramatic reading of a Shakespearian scene?

As ever, it all goes back to your formative assessment and decision as to where the students need to go next. You could mix up the abilities within the groups and give different tasks to specific students within the groups. This can be tricky and, as always, means you need to know the pupils well. Who will shrink back and find it difficult to contribute? Who will take it upon themselves to tell everyone what to do – even if they have no idea themselves? Who will take group work as an opportunity to muck about or chat about the latest gossip? Who will be willing to do the work of others in order to help the group succeed? Creating groups that help students try out different roles and not get stuck in their self-perceptions ('I'll colour in the title while you work out the hard bit') is important, if the activity is to help develop learning rather than reinforce stereotypes. One way to structure this is to give each student a specific task within the group; for example, note taker, timer, spokesperson, and so on.

Another version of organising group work that can be very helpful is the jigsaw (or snowball) technique.[13] The idea is that students are placed into 'home' groups and given a task to do, such as preparing a guide to weather systems. As this is a huge task, you then ask the students to move to their second grouping – topic (or expert) groups. These are groups made up of one or two students from each of the home groups who will work out the content for one area of weather systems. After a set time, you ring a bell and the students return to their home groups to share their knowledge. This has the advantage of ensuring all students play their part, and helps develop oracy and independent working.

Alternatively, you can break the class into groups depending on their level of understanding. So, more advanced students might need to apply their knowledge to a current event – for example, the impact of a mine closing on what is manufactured in a particular area. Or they could tackle word problems that use their ability to do multiplication of large numbers. Those who have struggled with the topic could create an aide memoire to help themselves in the future.

If you want to extend the students you can ask them to work in pairs, where one teaches the topic to the other. You want both students to really engage with the topic and feel positive about themselves, so you could give them both a few minutes to prepare. The 'teacher' could be directed to work out a visual way of explaining or a simple summary to help their 'pupil' and you could ask the recipient of the explanation to come up with three questions and perhaps a trick question to which they already know the answer to test their 'teacher'. You might want to ask the students to swap roles after a few minutes if you think it would be helpful.

The 'think, pair, share' or 'think, pair, square, share' technique asks students to discuss in pairs and then take their view to discuss in a larger group. This requires pupils to think quietly on their own, then move to a pair where they explain their idea and listen to their partner's thoughts. They can then be asked to join another pair (square) and again listen to the views of each person before deciding together which view or combination of ideas they will then share with the rest of the class.

The advantage of this is that many teachers will have either planned their seating plan in the classroom to accommodate this type of learning or will have allocated 'thinking partners', so the groupings are arranged – the only

---

[13] Jigsaw, snowball, marketplace activities, and home and expert groups are terms for very similar teaching techniques. See www.thinkinghistory.co.uk for a more thorough explanation of marketplace activities.

issue is what you will ask them to discuss. This system works because it encourages every student to join in at the paired stage and they then have something to offer in the larger group of four, or to the whole class.

The smaller the group and the shorter the activity, the more productive their work generally is. If you are planning a series of lessons using the same groups (such as may well happen in a drama lesson, for example), you will need to ensure that there is regular feedback on progress and set the next activity in the task accordingly. It is easy for lower-attaining or more withdrawn students to be lost in this type of work, so you may want to set up the task to ensure everyone has a role in the final activity and that this is recorded in some way.

It helps to give very clear expectations as to how the groups will work. You can break up the time allocated. ('You need to produce your ten-word definition in eight minutes. I will ring a bell to signal this.') Another way to do this is to show the class examples of the quality of work you are expecting them to produce in the next 30 minutes.

Breaking down the task

Breaking down the task can be done at a number of levels. At its most simple, it merely requires you to ask the student to do the first section of what you have asked the class to do, and then go back and check they have accomplished it and do any further explanations or reteaching as necessary before asking them to do the next section. This manoeuvre is actually very effective, and although it requires teacher input in the lesson, it does not take any preparation. However, it is difficult to carry out effectively if you have several pupils who need this. Of course, if they are working near each other, the organisation of this becomes much easier and you can teach several pupils at once.

If you have students in the class who will predictably struggle with a certain part of a task, you can build in a review activity before they start the section of the task that will cause them trouble: 'Do the first question, then look at the worked example on the sheet and copy it out into your book before doing question 2.' Or ask them to reread their homework on Martin Luther King's 'I have a dream' speech before writing a paragraph on his beliefs. You could ask pupils to complete the first part of the task and then raise their hand, when you will give them a stepping-stone activity to help them complete the more complex questions.

For older or higher-attaining students, it would be easy to write a list of resources they could consult on the board and refuse to answer any questions about what they are to do until they have read all of them (as illustrated in figure 9). For pupils who simply like the attention given by asking questions, you could use the system of letting them ask two or three questions only and, before you answer, ask them if this is worth using one of their questions on. With some students and groups I have reinforced this with counters to be 'spent'.

Some students may need the task adapting, as an instruction such as 'make notes' is too generalised for them to manage. In this case, it often only needs a reminder to clarify expectations and reassure. 'Read the first paragraph and write down one fact, and then read the second paragraph and write down a second fact. That should take about five minutes – then put up your hand and I will come and check and help you if needed.'

None of these ways of breaking down the task take more than a moment or two of preparation.

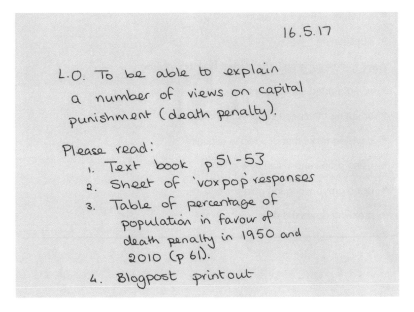

Figure 9: Example of a list of resources students should read before asking questions about a task or learning objective (LO)

How to

Changing the task

Setting appropriate tasks depends on being very clear about lesson aims and what students need to do next, as identified by formative assessment. You can do formative assessment by:

- walking around

- reading work

- quizzes

- student feedback

- activities within the lesson

- questioning.

Ways to adapt the task to different learners include:

- using graded success criteria

- adapting the speed of tackling the task

- devising tasks that develop in difficulty

- using props and visual aids

- using group work and paired work

- breaking down the task.

Chapter 4

Supporting sensory needs

Many people find they become easily overloaded by sensory input. This is a particular feature of autism spectrum disorder (ASD), but also affects other people. The impact of flickering lights or certain smells is much higher for them than it would be for most people. The opposite can also be true for some – they may be under-sensitive to external sensory input. Although we cannot always change the environment, we can very often ameliorate the situation so that the individual pupil can function well in the classroom.

Sensory difficulties include loss in one or more senses, so in this chapter I include advice on tweaking your teaching to support those with hearing and visual difficulties. The strategies regarding hearing benefit not only those who have a diagnosed hearing loss but also those who struggle with recurrent bouts of glue ear. The UK's National Health Service website suggests that eight out of ten children experience glue ear at least once in their childhood, and these episodes can last for a number of weeks. Visual difficulties can often be corrected by spectacles, but some children's problems cannot be corrected, for example, colour blindness.

We all absorb information through our senses, and so how the classroom is set out and used can improve the way learning takes place for all, but will have a greater impact on those with sensory needs. A good seating plan can enable you to place pupils in the optimum position for their learning and also provide a useful prompt to help you teach individuals in the way they learn best.

Some pupils with ADHD and some other difficulties fiddle with objects all the time. I have included some tips to accommodate this without distracting the rest of the class.

Differences in sensitivity

Pupils with ASD may have heightened sensitivity to sights, sounds, touch, smell, balance, and body awareness.[14] This can include sensitivity to light, fragmented images, distorted or muddled sounds, awareness of whispered or distant conversations, unwillingness to wear particular clothes, or touch certain surfaces. Sensitivity to smells can mean that being in canteens or laboratories is difficult. Also, some people struggle to be near those who wear perfume, or smell of garlic or 'coffee breath'.

Those with low sensitivities may enjoy noise and find it soothing, have very little sense of smell, hold others over-tightly, or be unaware of their positioning in relation to others and so become irritatingly close to them. This can mean that they may not acknowledge certain sounds and may be unaware of smells. Some children who are under-sensitive seek more stimulation – for example, by licking objects.

There are three main strategies for a class teacher to manage these difficulties:

- Be aware that some might experience the environment differently from you. Consider if there are ways you can improve the environment, for example by repairing electrical items that buzz or flicker. If you have personalised information about a pupil, you can adapt the classroom to help as far as possible. It may be that you can organise for students who struggle with these issues to eat somewhere else other than the canteen at lunch time – possibly with one or two friends. If that is not possible, perhaps they could have a seat saved for them at the edge of the dining area, where the noise and smells are likely to be diminished and they can easily leave if they need to.

- Prepare students who are sensitive to these issues if there are going to be activities that might be difficult for them to manage – for example, a science experiment or loud music. You can then discuss how to approach the situation. Often, just knowing about it, and having permission to leave the room and go to a pre-agreed quiet area if necessary, means that the event is much more manageable. The visual timetable explained in Chapter 7 will help the student prepare themselves.

- If you habitually plan a variety of activities, then there will probably be some time in each lesson when that student is more comfortable. For example, if you regularly have some silent working or reading time, those who find noisy situations exhausting or even distressing can relax and

---

[14] www.autism.org.uk/sensory (the website of The National Autistic Society).

focus on the task. If pupils work both in groups and independently at some point each day, it will give the students practice in social situations, as well as time to withdraw and recover.

Awareness of personal space

One sensory difficulty that many autistic children seem to experience is in being aware of others' body space. One tip for this is to teach them guidelines based on their outstretched arm. The space located from fingertips outwards is social space where it is acceptable to stand and talk to anyone. From the fingertips to elbow is a guideline for personal space where friends and those who are helping you can stand. From elbow to shoulder indicates private space where normally only family or partners enter without permission.[15] This needs introducing sensitively, as these 'rules' do not apply in queues and so on, and students can become very indignant if they feel the guidelines they have been taught are being broken. It helps to have an agreed place in a queue – either at the front (to reduce anxiety about their particular place being taken) or at the back, so as to avoid proximity to others. This is helpful for students who become very anxious if approached from behind.

Teaching strategies to help the hearing-impaired[16]

The term 'hearing-impaired' can cover those who have mild or significant hearing loss, intermittent hearing loss, and tinnitus. All those in this group may rely on a variety of strategies that you should include in your repertoire of teaching habits.

First, vision is important. The strategies mentioned in Chapter 1 all have their place. However, also make sure the pupil can see your face clearly. Teachers who wander around while speaking, or talk while writing on the board, can make it difficult for the pupil to lip read or use the teacher's expression to help give context to what they are saying. Make sure that the light is on your face rather than behind you. If you need to lower the lights, give any instructions before the lights go down so the pupil can see you as you are explaining what they need to do.

---

[15]I learned this strategy as part of Team-Teach training on positive responses to behaviours that challenge: www.teamteach.co.uk.

[16]See www.ndcs.org.uk (National Deaf Children's Society).

If you are using a video, use the subtitles feature to help understanding of the content.

Instructions, room changes, homework activities, and so on should be written on the board or recorded in another way. If the pupil mishears 'page thirty' for 'thirteen' the task will be completely confusing.

New vocabulary should also be given in a written form, as the pupil will not be able to recognise the word easily. It is very helpful if this can be reinforced by pictures so as to give context to help understanding.

Secondly, ensure the pupil is able to hear spoken information. If there is a question-and-answer session or a class discussion, it is helpful to repeat briefly each answer or point made. Although this slows down the pace of the lesson, it can also help those who have speech and receptive language difficulties. Be aware that if another pupil is reading from a textbook to the class, you may need to encourage them to raise the volume of their speech, as they may be too quiet. They do not need to shout or speak in an exaggerated way.

You may need to let the pupil know that they now need to listen by using their name, or even a light touch on the arm, if this has been agreed. Otherwise, general instructions to the whole class may pass by without the pupil realising their importance.

Lastly, be aware of how much the pupil is trying to accomplish. Those who have hearing impairment need to concentrate very hard to grasp what is being taught. This is also true if they are wearing hearing aids, because the sounds that are magnified are often unhelpful ones such as scraping chairs, background chat, and pen tapping. So it is very hard to do more than one task at a time, such as listen and make notes at the same time, or watch a video clip, read subtitles, and make notes all at once. It can really help to simply give a note of the video link or offer a copy of the slide presentation. Perhaps you could buddy the pupil up with someone who creates neat notes and give them access to a photocopier for easy copying.

Teaching strategies to help the visually impaired

One hopes that children with significant visual difficulties will have been diagnosed by the time they arrive at school and that those needing specific apparatus or accommodations will come with support and advice from external professionals. However, there are always children in school who have other issues that are not so significant but can cause problems for them. Again, the key is to know your pupils and to be aware of their needs.

One strategy that is helpful is to offer a commentary as you demonstrate an activity to students. Overt explanations of what you are doing, and why, give lots of clues to those who struggle to work out what they are expected to do if they have to rely on their impaired vision:

> As you draw the apparatus, you are not trying to do a 3D sketch, but a 2D diagram. This means it does not have to look lifelike, but you do want the larger pieces of equipment, such as the tripod, to be larger in your diagram. If you are not sure, go and have a closer look at the equipment on the side. Remember, all straight lines need to be drawn with a ruler.

Be willing to adjust the brightness of light in the classroom, as some pupils struggle with sunshine and others find working in darker conditions difficult (for instance, having to taking notes on a slide presentation when the blinds are down so as to see a screen better). If you cannot improve the situation, you can sometimes offer a quick, practical solution, such as a copy of the slides or photocopy of the notes, as you might for hearing-impaired students, thus reducing stress and the likelihood of tired eyes for the rest of the day.

For students with poor distance vision, you may need to offer reassurance and encouragement verbally rather than rely on smiles and glances across the room. They may also need to be alerted by name and specific instructions rather than gestures to tell them the next action expected of them. They will also need any information on the whiteboard to be written clearly and in large letters. It is important to keep the whiteboard clean – it is much harder to pick out information against a smeared, greyish background.

Strategies for those who are colour vision deficient (colour blind)

Up to 8.5 per cent of the world's population have colour vision deficiency, most of them male.[17] These difficulties range from very mild to a significant problem. Many people are not aware of their own difficulty. The most common form of colour vision deficiency is red/green colour blindness, but some people are blue/yellow colour blind.

---

[17] www.colourblindawareness.org.

This condition makes it difficult to accurately identify these colours in any form. So, for those with red/green colour blindness, the issue is relevant to any colour that has red or green as part of its composition. For example, comparing blue and turquoise (which contains some green) or blue and purple (which contains some red) would cause them problems. This means that those with colour blindness cannot rely on decisions based on colour, and, indeed, are often uninterested in colour.

In practical terms it means that activities that rely on colour alone are difficult. So instructions such as these are unhelpful: 'Pick up the purple bricks and put them in the red box.'; 'Place the recycling in the bin with green lid, not the brown one.'

The solution is to avoid identifying objects by colour alone: 'Pick up the smallest bricks – the purple ones – and put them in the red box by the door.'; 'Place the recycling in the bin with the green lid and a picture of a glass bottle on it, not the brown one – you will see that one is for plant waste if you open it.'

Avoid activities that can only be successfully completed by identifying colours. When working with younger pupils, be aware that some matching activities, games, and online activities are very dependent on colour. Older students may be reluctant to do colouring in case they inadvertently use the wrong colour and make the sky purple rather than blue. It helps to have coloured crayons labelled with their colour so that pupils who are old enough to read can choose by name as well as colour. It also helps them recognise what they see when others are referring to specific colours. Tasks that use colour-coding (for example, some tables and pie charts) can be improved by replacing or augmenting colours with stripes or dots or, at the very least, using bright primary colours rather than, for example, a pale pink that could be mistaken for white.

Consider your marking policy – does it rely on colours that are tricky to distinguish? Some schools use purple pens to mark, which some colour-blind pupils would struggle to distinguish from blue or black ink. Think about using symbols as well as colours to indicate what is good and unsatisfactory and how to improve it. Also, a marking policy that relies on highlighters can cause difficulties for some students who cannot see the yellow on white or distinguish between the yellow and orange or the green and blue.

Setting out the classroom to support those with sensory difficulties[18]

If you have the luxury of a classroom of your own, the way you organise it can have a powerful impact on how well pupils learn.

Avoid distraction

Set the classroom out so that – if at all possible – pupils are not distracted, either by what is behind you or by what is happening outside the window. (Once when I was teaching a lesson that was observed by another teacher a pigeon attacked and almost decapitated another bird on a flat roof next to the window. Half the class were fascinated and the other half horrified and trying not to vomit. As I said, try to avoid distraction.)

Think about where the door is in relation to your teaching space – have you set out the room so it is easy to enter discreetly during a lesson?

How noisy is the room? Can you reduce this in any way, such as putting rubber tips on chair legs if the floor is tiled? Think about whether you teach with the door open and how much this is affecting the noise level.

Line of sight

When you set out the classroom, sit wherever pupils will be and check their line of sight to the whiteboard or screen.

Interaction and grouping

As you decide where to place tables or desks, you need to think about how you want the students to interact with you and with each other. Do you want traditional rows with pupils seated in pairs, grouped together in sixes or eights, or perhaps in an arc facing you? There are positives and negatives for each style and I have swapped between them, depending on the groups I am teaching and the age of the pupils. The key is balancing pupils' ability to focus on you without having to twist around with the ease of working independently, as well as in the groups you find best for your class.

Your class seating plan can be a powerful tool to support the differentiation of learning. Think about whether you want different groups of similar ability

---

[18]www.asdteacher.com has useful advice on setting up the classroom for pupils with ASD.

working together (with the danger of students talking about others as being on the 'stupid table'). However, a potential benefit of this is that you can use any adult support in the classroom with a group instead of one-to-one. Also, those who are gifted and talented benefit hugely from the stimulus of others who can challenge their thinking or discuss the topic at a higher level. Many primary school classrooms organise the children into different groups for English and mathematics: this seems to work well and can reflect widely differing skills in these areas.

Mixed-ability seating can support those who struggle with their learning if the more advanced students are happy to help explain tasks and the ones who might struggle are willing to accept this. The challenge of explaining a task in a number of ways can itself be a good activity to help develop understanding. For example, asking a student to explain a task to someone else requires them to verbalise their understanding. If they have to break down the explanation into small steps, or change the analogy they are using, it means they now have a stronger grasp of the topic.

Placing individual pupils

As you plan where pupils are going to sit, think about those who have hearing loss in one ear and so need to sit to the right or left of you; those who are sensitive to light and so may struggle if the sun shines in their eyes; and so on. This detailed information may not be available on a register, but if you teach pupils old enough to write independently, you could start the academic year by asking them to fill in a short questionnaire about themselves. (When I have done this and included a question such as, 'what would you like to privately tell your teacher about yourself?' I always add the caveat that I might need to share the information with the safeguarding or child protection officer in school.) I have been amazed at the quality and detail of the information shared as part of this activity. Along with reminders about difficulties such as visual problems or reading, pupils have let me know about home situations and worries about learning about which the staff had no idea.

A seating plan that is annotated to remind you of specific strategies for particular students – and possibly some of the data you have on reading levels, target grades, or whatever is appropriate for the age and stage of your class – can be really helpful (figure 10). It is useful to keep the copies of these when data is updated or pupils are moved to new places, as they give a clear record of what strategies you have used and what works best for individual students.

Example of a seating plan

Sarah RA 12.4 1		Richie RA 13.8 G&T 1	Eric* RA 9.1 Fiddle object 4 Check hwk in planner
		Kate RA 13.1 G&T Deaf left ear 1	

Key

1–4:	different target grades and ability
	groups
anx:	anxious
col:	colour
hwk:	homework
E2L:	English as second language
G&T:	gifted and talented
GLD:	general learning difficulties
RA:	reading age
Sp&L:	speech and language difficulties
Specs:	spectacles
*:	potential pastoral needs

Manuel RA 10.6 Specs 3	Rana RA 10.9 Email hwk to parent 2	
Andy R.* RA 7.8 GLD 4	Mandy RA 8.2 Sp&L 4	Teacher's desk

Fred RA 10.3 Dyslexic? 12.1.17 Ask learning support team if any info 3	Mary RA 10.5 Specs 3
Andy P. RA 11.6 Col blind? 19.1.17 Discuss parents' evening 2	Bella* RA 11.3 Anx 2
Arjun RA 9.0 E2L Check hwk in planner 3	Louise RA 8.0 E2L Check hwk in planner 4

Figure 10: Example of a seating plan with explanatory notes

My class plans are normally scribbled on and scruffy with use. I would make sure that anything written is in my own code, so that if it is left open students cannot glean information on fellow pupils. The names written in italics (figure 10) have a learning needs profile that I need to refer to. An asterisk means that a pupil has been highlighted as potentially having pastoral needs based on financial difficulties or other issues. To explain the other notes:

- 'Check hwk in planner': I need to check this pupil has written their homework legibly in the planner

- 'Email hwk to parents': strategy requested by pastoral staff

- 'Col. blind?': a scribbled note that I have noticed a problem, when I noticed it, and what action I've taken or planned

- 'Dyslexic?': jotting that I have noticed possible dyslexic difficulties, when I noticed it, and what action I've taken or planned.

You could add in lots more information, such as target grades. Add information that will remind you of how to teach the students at a glance – it is your memory aid.

Displays

Most teachers take a pride in their classrooms and the displays around the walls. However, for students who can become overwhelmed by the sensory stimuli or who have visual difficulties, an area that is visually calm can be helpful. Also, if you are working with young children, try moving round the classroom at their level. Check you can see displays clearly. Sometimes, a display that is less exciting visually can be helpful, because it makes the main point extremely clear. Again, it is a matter of balance, because many students respond very well to bright and cheerful displays full of different textures and objects.

It helps students to work independently if you ensure that resources such as dictionaries or calculators are easily accessible and clearly labelled.

Teaching groups outside the classroom

If your role is to support small groups of pupils and you find yourself teaching anywhere, even the corridor or cloakroom, you will have to adapt the situation as best you can. I used to find that a small whiteboard easel is a helpful focus for the group. You can put it up anywhere and it sets a learning atmosphere. Also, having a bag to take with me containing clipboards, paper, pens and pencils and mini whiteboards and pens meant I could approximate a reasonable teaching environment pretty well anywhere without too much bother.

Fiddle objects

Many people fiddle with objects when they concentrate, perhaps twiddling a pencil, clicking a pen, or doodling. Some pupils, if they have nothing to fidget with, may pick at scabs, or do other harmful things, or really struggle to concentrate.

However, there are two problems with anything that anybody twiddles with. One is the potential to distract or irritate others, and the other is the potential to distract themselves. Many students argue indignantly that they need a fiddle object to help them concentrate. This, in their view, seems to justify playing with tiny skateboards or creating little models with modelling clay. The fact that they have been so absorbed in their own activity that they have missed the lesson content seems irrelevant to them.

One possibility is to offer the students something silent to fiddle with – nothing that rattles or taps, and preferably out of sight so as not to distract others. Squeeze balls or a piece of textured material taped under the desk to brush their finger over can work well. An unblown-up balloon is satisfyingly stretchy. A good fiddle object should be small enough to fit in a fist, inexpensive, have no potential for rattling or clicking, and carry no inherent temptation (such as bouncy balls or rubber bands – easy to flick at someone 'by mistake'). They should be easy to keep out of eyeline under the desk so as not to distract other pupils.

A conversation setting out the expectation of keeping these objects silent, out of sight, and why this is important for other pupils will give you a clearly understood basis for the reminders that are likely to be frequently needed.

Another possibility is to teach the students to do something that needs no props and offers the repetitive movement that seems to help them focus – such as twiddling their thumbs.

Some people concentrate better when doodling – but again, you need to know your pupils. For some, the drawing helps them focus on listening and so a notebook for this purpose can be offered, especially for the teacher-talk section of the lessons. For others, the doodling becomes an end in itself and absorbs them – this is clearly not enabling them to learn better.

Opportunities to move around

Most people do not learn well if they have been sitting in the same position for a long time. It makes sense for you to build in opportunities for your pupils to move. This could involve changing from one seating position to another (such as from the carpet to tables for young children or into discussion groups for older students) or moving to collect resources. You could do an activity where students show their view on a subject or statement by standing in a line that stretches from 'I agree' at one side of the classroom to 'I disagree' at the other. Or you could do a quick quiz with yes or no answers – those who agree stand up and those that disagree crouch down. If there is no logical option for moving during a long teaching session, it can often help to get the whole class on their feet and do a few stretches. It gives an opportunity to open a few windows and stir the class into improved concentration.

Try to give pupils with hyperactive conditions extra opportunities to move, such as handing out books or collecting up paper into the recycling bin. It gives you the opportunity to thank them, which is much better than being tempted to rebuke them for what feels like excessive fidgeting.

How to

Supporting sensory needs

- Be aware of differences in sensitivity and manage difficulties by:

  - adapting the environment where possible

  - preparing students for activities they may find difficult

  - planning a variety of activities so each student has some times when they are more comfortable

- Teaching strategies to help hearing-impaired pupils

- Teaching strategies to help visually impaired pupils

- Strategies to help colour-blind pupils

- Setting out the classroom to accommodate sensory needs

  - avoid distraction

  - think about line of sight

  - manage interaction and grouping

  - keep seating plans and update them

  - use displays carefully

- Teaching groups outside the classroom

- Using fiddle objects

- Increasing opportunities for pupils to move around.

Chapter 5

Marking

As David Didau[19] helpfully explains, good marking is personalised differentiation. Each pupil will be given an individual response based on their needs. The trick is how to do this so that students understand what they have done well and what the next step is for them without the teacher spending hours and hours on the task. Any time that teachers put into marking should pay back in enabling students to learn better.

So what is good marking? Good marking will do one or more of the following:

- The teacher will be aware of which pupils have successfully completed the task and which need to be followed up because there is a problem with their work.

- The teacher will know what needs teaching and how in the next lesson (formative assessment).

- The teacher will know how well the pupils have performed against objective criteria (summative assessment).

- The learner will know that the teacher has acknowledged their work is satisfactory.

- The learner will know what they have done or understood correctly.

- The learner will know how to improve their work.

- The learner feels motivated and encouraged to work.

- Pupils who have learned the topic or skill quickly and accurately are pointed towards ways of applying or extending their knowledge.

Experienced teachers will have established a pattern for marking that works within their school's marking policy. For those new to teaching, in this chapter I give some general guidance and then explain the different purposes of marking and how these can be

---

[19] David Didau's blog is full of excellent ideas: www.learningspy.co.uk.

accomplished – and even possibly save some time. I also consider the benefits of peer marking and triple impact marking. The last part of the chapter focuses on different ways to support those with a variety of needs or who need a challenge to develop their work.

Prompt marking

It is helpful to mark work promptly for all pupils, but especially those who have memory difficulties. The longer the gap between completing the work and responding to it, the less useful the task becomes. You need to think carefully about when you have time to mark and, if possible, take account of this in how you schedule activities that will be marked, although this does not always work and every teacher has faced a depressingly huge pile of marking every now and again.

Clear, legible and respectful marking

The most important aspect of any marking is that it should be easily understood by the student. As most marking is done by hand, this means that your handwriting must be legible, especially to those who struggle to read. I tend to print any comments for those who have reading difficulties, but must confess that students occasionally push an exercise book in front of me and ask what I have written. If you teach younger children, you might read out comments as you go round the classroom. It is still useful to write them as a record of what you want to let them know – but ensure this is not a wasted effort.

Most schools use marking symbols, such as underlining a word and writing 'sp' in the margin to indicate a spelling mistake. The meaning of these needs specifically teaching to students so they can respond as required. For those who find reading difficult, it is helpful to limit the number of symbols you use in each piece of work.

I also think marking should model what we expect of students. Books with 'unfinished' scrawled over them in scruffy writing – while an understandably frustrated response – will be unlikely to elicit neat and careful work. Comments should be courteous and state your expectations. If at all possible, include a positive comment before a negative one. Using the student's name seems to increase the impact of the statement and the likelihood of it being complied with gracefully: 'Andrew, improved presentation. Complete section C at break time.'; 'Georgia, you have included a clear explanation on your view in first paragraph. A second paragraph with another viewpoint needed.'

If you feel the work is extremely poor, then a comment on previous positive achievements can be helpful before explaining what is unacceptable and what should now be done: 'Marina, your answers in the lesson showed excellent understanding. I was disappointed that you only answered two questions. Please see me to discuss.'

If your memory is as poor as mine, you need to mark with your planner or diary open in front of you so you can briefly record who you need to speak to or follow up in the next lesson. If pupils have been absent for some of the working or preparation time for a task, you could ask them to note it at the top of their work so you can take it into account when marking. This takes away anxiety and they sometimes offer to put in extra time to catch up.

What is the purpose of your marking?

Formative assessment

If you are simply checking the work has been done and there are no misunderstandings or errors that need to be tackled in future lessons, then a stamp ('checked by teacher') or tick should be sufficient.

However, formative marking can be detailed. This should be linked to the aim of the piece – the success criteria. Sharing this with students before they do the task can be useful, so they know what they are aiming at. Giving very specific guidelines is not always helpful, though, especially if you have set a more open, creative task. We want pupils to be able to think independently and reach conclusions in their own way. It can also narrow down what students feel confident to produce. Also, success criteria are not always available, for example in examinations.

However, as a teacher, you should have a very clear idea of what you want the students to achieve. What do you want them to be able to explain, calculate or demonstrate? What do you want them to be able to do (and crucially, repeat at a later date)?

It is always important to indicate what has been correct or been done to a good standard. How will pupils know this, as well as what has not worked and that they need to correct? If the work does not fit a simple system of ticks and crosses (or dots if you dislike crosses), this could be indicated by underlining good work and highlighting what needs improving or correcting (so as to be very clear for colour-blind students, many of whom find it difficult to distinguish between different coloured highlighters). This does involve having two pens and swapping them over – I would avoid any more than two, having tried a marking system that involved several and became hopelessly confused, as well as struggling to have all the requisite pens in one place when I settled down to mark.

Some schools use a system of a double tick in the margin to indicate a good example of whatever is the focus of learning, or a star stamp. A comment can be added to specifically explain why, if you wish.

Summative assessment

This will result in a mark or grade that will be recorded. The actual marking might look similar in most ways to a detailed piece of formative assessment marking, but you will be checking the work against some sort of mark scheme.

Marking for motivation and behaviour

Comments that positively affirm the learning behaviour you want can be very powerful. Looking through exercise books to check work has been completed can be used as an opportunity to write individual comments on the pupils' attitudes to work to encourage a positive attitude. This can work very well for a large class when you are aware you have not spoken at length to a number of pupils, or with a class that has been disaffected. I have noticed that students have referred back to these comments months later and have really taken them to heart. The behaviour of the class normally improves significantly for a while afterwards too. Comments could include phrases such as:

- I noticed you put up your hand several times last lesson. Well done.

- I have noticed that you have been checking spellings in the dictionary. Good to see.

- I really like the way you are willing to ask questions about the tricky bits of this topic. You are helping lots of people in the class by doing this.

Approaches that can save time when marking

Self-assessment

This is an extremely useful strategy for certain sorts of work as children get older. You can simply give out the marking schemes and ask the students to work out their own mark or underline correct information they have included in their answer. However, this can be a tricky activity for some. If it is not well managed it simply reinforces feelings of hopelessness and demotivates. So what can be done to make the activity helpful and meaningful?

One way is to slim down the marking scheme for this group so, for example, they are only marking for content. Another possibility is to ask them to mark positively; that is, underline or highlight anything they have included that is mentioned in the mark scheme. You could also ask them to identify one or two more elements to improve their answer.

Marking during the lesson

Marking while a task is in progress is an extremely effective use of time, as you can redirect pupils or correct misunderstandings before they reinforce their mistakes in their written work. Also, you can encourage and motivate by pointing out specific aspects of their work that have improved or are correct. This is a wonderful opportunity to challenge those who are coping easily with the task and develop the difficulty of the task for them. For those who are struggling, you can break down the task and perhaps write a correct example in their books as guidance.

Sometimes I go round a class and just put a dot by anything that needs to be corrected or improved. You might decide to ask students to write down your advice. I rarely ask students to do this, as it can interrupt their flow of thought and can be tricky for those who have literacy or handwriting difficulties, but occasionally it can reinforce the correction of a habitual mistake.

Some schools use a stamp marked 'verbal feedback' to show the teacher has given this input. I am not sure how this helps the student, but it can be useful evidence that you discuss the pupils' work with them if that is required in your setting.

Marking using improvement codes

As you mark a piece of work, you can save time by flicking through a few books and noticing what the pupils need to do to improve their work. You then give each strategy to improve their work a number code and, before the next lesson, write the codes and explanations on the board or screen. You then simply go through the books and allocate one or more codes to each student. You can, of course, differentiate by making some responses very straightforward activities and others more advanced research or a response to a provocative question. In the next lesson, ask all the pupils to copy down the required response linked to their code and then complete it.

Crib sheet

I cribbed this idea from @MrThorntonTeach.[20] You create a format for your subject or class (figure 11) and then, as you read through the work, you write all your comments on the crib sheet, which you then photocopy and hand to each student. I normally photocopy mine on bright yellow paper, which makes it easy to find in a folder or exercise book.

History Marking Crib Sheet	Date:	Class:
Praise:	Missing/Incomplete Work:	SPaG:
Even Better If:	Presentation & GMS:	DIRT Activities: Consolidate
Misconceptions:		Develop
		Stretch
Actions:	Polaroid Moments:	

KEY
SPaG: Spelling and grammar
GMS: Growth mindset
DIRT: Directed improvement and response time

Figure 11: Greg Thornton's crib sheet template, by permission of the author

The crib sheet should contain a box for common misunderstandings to correct with the class, reasons to praise specific people for specific points, and activities to improve the work (including some extension tasks). Figure 12 shows an example of a crib sheet I used with a class of 15–16-year-olds. I adapted Greg Thornton's template for a mock examination (noting, for example, who had done particular questions well, and making sure that everyone was included somewhere on the list). When I trialled this, I reckoned it saved me between half and two thirds of my normal allotted marking time.

---

[20] The @MrThorntonTeach twitter feed and blog, mrthorntonteach, have given me lots to think about and ideas to use.

Marking sheet – Year 11 Option D	(Letters in brackets refer to section of question)
Excellent answers Q1 Lauren (a) (c) Ellie (b) Molly (c)	**Misunderstandings to correct in class** • Quaker views of rights of embryo • Catholic views on divorce & remarriage
Excellent answers Q2 Frankie (b) Molly (b) Chris (b) Lauren (c) Ellie (c)	• Adoption ≠ surrogacy • Non-voluntary euthanasia
Excellent answers Q3 Alex (a) Josh (d) Frankie (c) Lauren (b) Phoebe (c) Ben (d) Phoebe (d) Ellie (d) Abi. H. (d)	**Common spelling or grammatical mistakes** integrate fundamental belief disagree (not ss) capital letters for Christian, Bible, Old/New Testament NB Readability of handwriting
Excellent answers Q4 Josh (c) Molly (b) Chris (a) Lauren (b) Ben (b) - esp definition	
Excellent answers Q5 Alex (b) Ellie (b)(c) (d) Ben (d) Molly Maria (b)	**Ways to gain marks** • A2c Comment on different sources for somatic cell therapy • Check you number 'B' questions correctly
Excellent answers Q6 Phoebe (b) Lauren (a) (c) Kate(a)(c) Harry (b) (a)	• A1(a) Look at picture giving hint • Often useful to define subject
Grade levels E 37 A* 69 F 30 A 63 g 23 B 57 C 51 D 44 Exam out of 76	• Specific phrases / words • Write four point answer as paragraph, not list. • Check answers relevant to question.

Figure 12: Example of a completed crib sheet for a mock examination

Self-checking before marking

It is reasonable practice to ask that work is checked and standard errors are corrected before marking. Older pupils should check that capital letters and full stops have been use properly, for example. Diagrams should have a title neatly underlined. Mathematics answers may need to indicate whether the measurements are in centimetres or metres. If the students assure you that the work has been checked, but clearly has not, you will need to have a system for dealing with it. One teacher I know gives two chances and then requires that the whole piece is redone – and this for seven-year-olds (albeit those who are competent readers and writers). Having struggled for years to get some 16-year-olds, who know perfectly well how to write sentences, to include capital letters and full stops, I now agree with this hard-line attitude, as we are not doing anyone any favours by letting students develop poor habits that will cause problems for a lifetime.

How could you adapt this expectation for students who are going to find some of the usual requirements difficult? To some extent, it is even more important that you help them set good habits in place – if the work has taken more effort to create, it makes sense that you help them make sure this is not wasted. However, this obviously needs to be done with sensitivity as to what is reasonable.

Some teachers have created a stamp where the student has to tick the relevant sections and sign to say they have done this. You could easily adapt this for specific students. In the example shown in figure 13, you could write in an individual instruction in the blank row and cross out any that are not the current focus of effort and support.

CAPITAL LETTERS	
FULL STOPS	
SUBJECT WORD SPELLINGS	
TITLE AND DATE UNDERLINED	
SIGNED	

Figure 13: Example of ink stamp for self-checking work

For example, you might cross out 'title and date underlined' for a pupil who struggled to manipulate a ruler. For another student you could ask that they number each question in the margin and add this in the blank row.

Peer marking: why, why not and how to use it effectively

Peer marking for simple tests with one correct answer per question can be usefully done as you go through the test in class. Apart from this purpose, it took me years to work out the point of peer marking. I would ask pupils to peer mark their partner's work and they would invariably praise it (often inappropriately if it was poor work) and frequently try to correct spellings (often wrongly and occasionally crossing out correct spellings and replacing them with incorrect ones) and suggest something to improve it – this was the more helpful response, but still the cause of many misunderstandings. So how can you use peer marking productively?

Awareness of how others have tackled the work

It helps students to look at other people's work. For pupils with learning difficulties it helps them see several versions of what they are attempting and pick up some ways of working that might be helpful. As they look at others' work and ask questions about it, they can learn more about how to do it themselves.

So to do this, you can set up a lesson where pupils wander round the class and look at two or three pieces of work done by other students. You can give them a piece of scrap paper to take with them to jot down any content or ways of working they would like to use themselves. They then go back to their own work and improve it with the suggestions they have gleaned.

This is fairly easily differentiated by asking the students who might be overwhelmed by the task to look at two specific pieces of work and answer a specific question, such as 'how did they begin their first paragraph?' For students who are working at the more-able end of the spectrum, you could ask them to spot the most common mistakes or omissions and report back (without using any names). This can help the more able to be more aware of what makes a good piece of work. Alternatively, you could ask them to look at some examples of work from the year groups above and ask them to identify positive aspects they could emulate.

Peer evaluation through questions

This is not really peer marking; it is learning through discussion. You can differentiate this type of task by asking some pupils to look at two or three pieces of work done by other students and come up with questions to ask about it. Others may need you to suggest the questions to ask other students. Still others will need one or two questions and then will be able to create their own.

Peer evaluation example questions

- 'Why do you set the calculation out like that?'

- 'Where is north on this map?'

- 'How did you show that the fox is terrified?'

- 'What type of ethical approach does this show?'

Peer evaluation through marking monitors

Another way to help students gain a deeper understanding of what they are aiming for is to use the monitor system. In this you nominate one or two pupils to be monitors for a particular skill you want to see embedded into the class's work. This could, for example, be using adjectives or setting out calculations so the decimal point is in the correct place. They then are given five minutes at a specified moment to wander round the classroom offering house points or smiley faces to any student who has met these criteria. If you choose pupils who need to use this skill themselves, you are getting them to see it in others' work again and again.

Pupils seem to like having special badges or lanyards to indicate their status (even as mid-teenagers).

Peer evaluation through being teaching assistants

Thank you to David Didau[21] for this idea. This is when one or two students who are struggling with the task accompany you around the room as you mark and talk through the work with those students who are one step ahead of them. You then ask the student(s) to do the next conversation, following your example. After ten minutes or so, you can then ask them how they are going to improve their work when they go back to their seat.

Peer evaluation using sentence starters

This is a more traditional way of peer marking. Students read through another person's work and use given sentence starters to comment on it.

---

21 www.learningspy.co.uk.

Examples could include a positive response, something to praise (linked to the assessment criteria or learning focus of the task), and something to work on – you could give a list of suggestions to choose from.

Example sentence starters

Positive responses:

- The section I thought worked best is…
- When I read this I learned…
- I like…

Something to praise:

- You have explained…
- You used a variety of…

Something to work on:

- Include an explanation of the quotation in paragraph…
- Include three more…
- Rewrite the… so that…

Ensuring a positive response to others' work

This is taught by the teacher through ground rules that are strictly reinforced. No one is allowed to be rude about another's work. In the strategies above, I would pair up or group students very carefully and only allow those I could trust to wander the room. If I was slightly unsure, I would take them with me on a teaching assistant tour and ask them guided questions such as, 'What is good about the way she has set out the diagram?' to ensure polite responses.

Time for students to improve work

Some schools call this DIRT (directed improvement and response time). This is also sometimes described as a learning relationship within an exercise book that should enable the student to develop their understanding and skills. Anyone looking at the book can see their development.

What could you ask students to do in the time given for improving their tasks?

- Complete any work that remains unfinished.

- Extend writing on a topic or prompt given by you – you could draw a box to indicate how much writing you are expecting.

- Redo a section or set of questions that are incorrect (with guidance as to which page of the textbook to use to help them).

- Answer a question to extend their work if what has been done so far is satisfactory.

- Ask them to work in a small group with either the teacher or support adult to correct misunderstandings.

It is worth checking briefly if what you have asked for has been done – the easiest way to do this is to set a plenary activity at the end of the time and quickly walk round the classroom checking books with a marking pen to tick work or stamper in hand. Otherwise, all you have done is create yet another set of marking to go through.

Triple impact marking[22]

This is a system that helps to improve the pupil's work using a triple-layered approach. It can be used for both formative and summative assessment, as shown in figure 14. The approach has identified lots of different ways teachers can interact with learners to improve their work. Some combine some of the suggestions I've already outlined. For example:

1. Students proofread their work by checking that they have completed the set tasks, it is set out according to the guidelines you have given, and they have included grammatical marks and correct spellings.

2. The teacher checks that the students have proofread the work (and sends it back if not) and provides feedback.

3. Students then practise the teacher's suggestions.

Another version of this could be:

1. Students proofread their work.

2. Students improve their work after referring to a correct or excellent version of the work, using a different-colour pen.

3. The teacher checks the work is proofread and has been improved in some way and gives one more suggestion to improve it further.

Yet another version:

1. Students proofread their work and highlight a particular section for which they would like feedback.

---

[22] Developed by Clevedon School, England. David Didau discusses the approach at www.learningspy.co.uk.

2 The teacher checks they have proofread the work (and sends it back if not) and provides feedback on the highlighted section.

3 Students then practise the teacher's suggestions.

This version also means that as a teacher you do not need to mark page after page of closely written work – you only mark a short section of it (as well as briefly checking it has been proofread in line with your expectations for that particular pupil).

There are numerous versions of triple impact marking, some of which have become very complex. However, if used in a simple version, it is very useful. It assumes that the student has the responsibility for handing in the best work they can, and drills in the importance of good practice, such as setting out maths questions properly or using correct grammar. Some versions help students develop skills in editing and improving work or checking for an accurate process against an exemplar.

This system should build in differentiation, because your suggestions will lead on from the work the student has done.

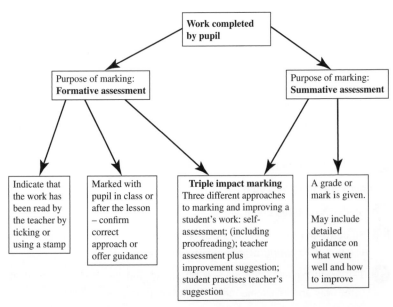

Figure 14: Types of marking for formative and summative assessment

Awareness of students with specific difficulties

You will hopefully be aware of the students in the group who have fine motor difficulties and struggle to present their work neatly, or those who take extra time to think through a sentence before writing it down, and so complete less work than others. It helps in these cases to praise effort and small steps. Sometimes I ask students to see for themselves how they have progressed over time by asking them to compare a good piece of work to their first piece of work in their exercise book. They are very often gratified and encouraged, and as a result are happy to keep putting in the effort to make the next small improvement.

Are you going to correct every single spelling mistake and write it out for the student to use to write out three times? I recommend varying your practice, depending on the learner's needs. Clearly, a severely dyslexic student would have their work completely covered in corrections if you did this. In this case, I would focus on two or three spelling mistakes – possibly subject-specific words that are not too complex.

On the other hand, if I was a class teacher and knew exactly which spellings the pupil had been working on in extra support classes, I would want to spot whether they had managed them accurately in their classwork (if so, congratulations would be in order) and if not, ask the pupil to practise them again. However, students who are perfectly able to copy the spelling of subject-specific words from the textbook and have not bothered to do so should be taken to task, and I would expect them to correct each mistake. You can change your expectations to suit the student.

Awareness of students who are more or the most able in the group

Marking is a golden opportunity to challenge and stretch those who have grasped the learning easily. Questions and challenges can be included to follow up, either in lesson time, or later on in their own time. Asking students to justify their answers or explain how this topic links to another given subject can introduce depth and breadth in their learning. A challenge to research which authors have also used similes and metaphors based on how animals behave or weather patterns could both extend knowledge and spark interest in different genres of fiction or poetry. This is personalised differentiation that takes no longer than writing one line in an exercise book.

How to

Marking

- Prompt marking
- Clear, legible and respectful marking
- What is the purpose of your marking?
  - formative assessment
  - summative assessment
  - marking for behaviour and motivation
- Approaches that save time
  - self-assessment
  - marking during lessons
  - marking using improvement codes
  - crib sheets
  - self-checking before marking
- Peer marking and how to use it effectively:
  - awareness of how others have tackled the work
  - peer evaluation through questions
  - peer evaluation through marking monitors
  - peer evaluation through being teaching assistants
  - peer evaluation through using sentence starters
  - ensuring a positive response to others' work
- Time for students to improve their work
- Triple impact marking
- Awareness of students with specific difficulties
- Awareness of students who are more or the most able in the group.

Chapter 6

Using other people to support differentiation

E very teacher of a class has a number of people who can support differentiation in the classroom. For some teachers this will be the students and their parents or carers. Others are able to call on other adults such as learning support staff, working either in the class, or one-to-one or with small groups outside the classroom.

Any supporters you have can help by doing regular activities such as reading, or precision teaching, or acting as mentors.

Parents and carers are often extremely keen to help, but are sometimes unsure as to how to do this. Schools that enable and empower them to support their children effectively will find the investment of effort and time very worthwhile.

Support staff such as learning support assistants (LSAs) are able to offer invaluable support both within and outside lessons.

Reading practice

Volunteer students and support adults can offer this alongside parents and carers listening to the child read at home.

Many educationalists have been inspired by the 'Each One Teach One' idea pioneered by Frank Laubach,[23] which has led to various paired reading initiatives. One example is the UK scheme developed by the National Literacy Trust.[24] Students who have become good readers can volunteer to be a peer tutor for another student. This involves some training for the tutors (which can have all sorts of positive side effects on both their own reading and also their parenting later in life). They then meet with their tutees to read together up to two or three times per week, thus offering a huge amount of extra one-to-one reading time.

Depending on the age and stage of the pupils receiving the support, the tutors could use the paired reading ideas in Chapter 2.

If students are to do this, they will need supervision, as some 'tutors' will easily fall back into the habits of telling their 'tutees' what the word is that they are struggling with, rather than encouraging them to break it down, and so on. Also, there is the potential for bossy behaviour to take place if not carefully managed. However, when this type of scheme works well, it has wonderful benefits.

The idea as developed by the National Literacy Trust is to develop the scheme school-wide. However, it would be perfectly possible to do within a class or tutor group with the teacher circulating the pairings so as to hear each pairing read regularly. Doing it this way, you could also use the paired reading time to pre-teach (teach pupils about topics and vocabulary coming up in the syllabus before the class study them) or review vocabulary studied within class (overlearning) as well as reading books. The key to using the pairings for effective differentiation, as so often, is communication. If you can get copies of subject word lists to each volunteer (especially if it is a photocopy of the one the pupil created), they can help the pupil learn vocabulary.

If you are encouraging the pupil to use a dictionary, make sure the volunteer knows this and has a copy of the same edition used in the classroom to

---

[23]**F. Laubach** (1960). *Toward World Literacy: The Each One Teach One Way*. Syracuse University Press.

[24]www.literacytrust.org.uk.

hand. You could ask a volunteer to run through a version of the alphabet song with the learner or play some numeracy games to back up the work in lessons.

Some schools use community volunteers or non-teaching staff, asking lunchtime supervisors, administrators and so on to offer a little extra time to help improve reading by listening to readers. All of these ideas have great merit as long as the volunteers are carefully trained and are used consistently. The volunteers need to work with the same learner at least weekly. Also, the volunteers need to fit in with the school's chosen terminology when discussing phonics – for example, if the school uses terms such as digraph to refer to two letters that have one sound (such as 'th'), then everyone working with the pupil needs to refer to them similarly.

I think the easiest way to communicate between the teacher and volunteer is to have some sort of joint record such as a notebook or shared record sheet, which could easily be online. It is helpful to ask for specific information and this will need modelling – you could offer a good example with the names blocked out. It would be good practice to ask the pupil being supported for their views and include them also. All of this does take a little time, but it is worth the investment, as a trained volunteer is a long-term resource who may support many pupils over the months and years.

A record of support should be kept and can be completed as the session occurs (table 5). Comments such as 'worked well' or 'refused to work' are not very informative. The more specific the information is, the better – especially if other staff members need to take over a session, or use the information to discuss with parents, or to give evidence that more or less support is required.

It is also helpful to find out which volunteers will work well with students with advanced interests in specific subjects such as rocketry or engineering. They may be able to encourage learners in subjects in which you have little or no expertise. Perhaps they could share websites or pass on magazines to encourage reading.

Table 5: Example of learning support session log kept by a volunteer or support staff

Name of child: FW Staff: GC Volunteer: NB		
Learning target: To spell one-syllable words containing blends (sn, sl, sp, sk, sc) To read a level 2 book independently		
Resources: foam letters, word list, blends game, reading book		
Date	**Supporter comment**	**Pupil comment**
2/3/17	*Able to blend when writing words after two practices using foam letters but stumbled over examples in reading book.*	I am bored with this book.
9/3/17	*Able to blend when writing words after one practice and could identify 'sp' in spot without any support.*	I like my new book better. My Mum thinks my reading is improving.
16/3/17	*Able to blend when writing words after one practice and could identify 'sp' in spot without any support. Note – upset as pet dog poorly.*	I think my reading is getting better but I didn't want to come to school today as Fluffy is poorly.
23/3/17	*Able to blend foam letters without any help and could use 'sp', and 'sn' in word writing but struggled with 'sl'. Note – request hearing check – does not seem to be hearing ends of words well.*	I finished the book. I got a sticker.

Precision teaching[25]

Again, this is support that can be provided by volunteer students, adult supporters, and parents and carers, as long as they are clear about how this session should be run.

This is a way of learning sight knowledge of common vocabulary and numeracy facts. The chosen words or facts are written one per card and the adult goes through them in random order, helping the child read them and putting them into sentences or demonstrating the number facts with cubes. The cards are then shuffled and the pupil attempts to read as many as possible correctly or answer as many calculations as possible in one minute without any adult help. This accuracy rate is recorded. This activity is repeated daily

---

[25]A helpful guide to precision teaching can be found at www.sendgateway.org.uk. Other publications about programmes with similar methods include *Toe by Toe* by Keda and Harry Cowling and *Power of 2: The One to One Coaching System for Maths* by David Joseph Sharp.

until the pupil has a secure knowledge of the chosen words or numeracy facts. The advantage of this is that is takes a short time (about 15 minutes in total) and progress can be demonstrated as the accuracy level increases.

Mentors

Older students and, sometimes, community or school staff volunteers can be mentors to younger pupils. Mentoring tends to focus on motivation, self-esteem and supporting positive behaviour.

These pairings can be extremely beneficial. Training should be offered, for example, in listening techniques, and clear expectations and guidelines should be set. Mentors may well need some support themselves, especially if they are supporting young people with significant difficulties and issues, and this needs to be considered when setting up the scheme. While some degree of privacy and confidentiality can be expected by the mentees, it must be clear that any concerns about pupil safety will be passed on to the relevant staff members.

These schemes need to be a school-wide initiative to work well and maintain the training and supervision required to keep them positive and focusing on the outcomes set. However, teachers who have worked with mentors in both primary and secondary settings have reported that pupils who have trained as mentors have experienced increased success in their own academic achievements and self-management of behaviour.

How to involve parents and carers in supporting differentiation

Most younger children take reading books home, and very often homework also. Parents and carers get drawn into helping with these. It is really helpful if guidance can be offered by the school, especially on how the children are expected to set out their calculations or how to do reading support. As a class teacher, it really helps if you can set up the expectation that parents and carers can jot down what the child has succeeded at and where the difficulties lie, and you will help resolve any concerns. A short conversation like this at parents' evening or consultation can pay back many times over in your knowledge of the pupil and in the support you will receive from home.

Most parents and carers really want to help. Asking them to do a clearly explained task with the child for ten minutes every day, such as a precision-teaching sheet or three pages of paired reading, may be more motivating than vague expectations of listening to reading. It is worth sourcing helpful video clips to put on the school website to demonstrate how to do paired reading or set out calculations.[26] Be aware that there are likely to be parents who themselves struggle with reading because of their own additional needs or because English is a second or third language they are still acquiring.

Working with colleagues to differentiate within the classroom

Colleagues within the classroom such as LSAs offer excellent support. Most LSAs have extremely detailed knowledge of the children they work with and can offer the teacher helpful information and insights into difficulties the child is experiencing and the most productive way of overcoming them. Some schools ask LSAs to create or contribute to pen portraits of the students (figure 15), which can be then kept centrally. These are useful for all students, not just those identified as having an additional need.

Support staff in the classroom are not there to make things easy for the learner (or the teacher), but to enable the learner to succeed. What strategies can they use to do this when working with individuals or small groups?

Checking understanding

Check the pupil's understanding of the task by asking them to explain back to the adult what they have been asked to do. The adult can then clarify any misunderstandings. Using a mini whiteboard to jot down the task is helpful, even if it has been displayed on the board or interactive whiteboard. It means the pupil can point to the section they do not understand and an explanation can be given.

Breaking down the task

Sometimes the additional adult can break down the task a stage further than the teacher. For example, they might look at text with a pupil and ask the pupil to read it out loud and then read it silently. Or perhaps the pupil could be asked to write down what they know about a particular topic before tackling the scaffolded task so the adult and student can discuss together which piece of information is required. They might ask questions about

---

[26]There is a wealth of videos on YouTube: search, for example, 'paired reading'. www.mathmeeting.com is a helpful source of mathematics videos.

Pen portrait

Pupil: Chloe J.　　Year: 7　　Age: 12.01　　Reading age: 10.01

Form tutor: EH　　LSA: FB　　Date: 2/6/2017

Chloe is a friendly and popular girl. She enjoys looking after her pets and is very knowledgeable about different breeds of dogs. She often gives constructive verbal contributions to lessons.

When asked to complete a written task she will spend a long time preparing and writing the title and avoids actually writing. She often presents as being overwhelmed by the task.

Chloe has reading difficulties but no specific diagnosis of dyslexia or similar. She often confuses short words that look similar, e.g. what and when.

When copying a long number, Chloe often muddles the order of the numerals.

Suggested strategies:

1) Reread text with her if possible.
2) Ensure she has a key word list on the desk.
3) Break down the task – especially the first section.
4) Ask Chloe to write on alternate lines so corrections can be clearly written above the word.
5) Offer scaffolded tasks.
6) Encourage her to have a go and not to worry about spellings on her first draft.
7) Send copies of key word list to FB before the topics are taught so they can be pre-taught.
8) Use exercise books with large squared paper for numeracy tasks so she can write one numeral per square.

Any comments or suggestions to FB to collate, please.

Figure 15: Example pen portrait

the process: 'How will you do this calculation?'; 'How will you check your answer?' Sometimes the teacher will have gauged the level of work wrongly and the LSA can quietly adapt the task to suit the individual student.

Developing self-help skills

An LSA is in a prime position to help the student develop better self-help skills. The most wonderful colleagues I have worked with seem to be far harder on the students than I am, because they know what the student is capable of and are willing to push them to achieve it. They can remind the student to use the word list, scaffolding sheet, or multiplication square – and, of course, praise them when they do this independently. They can ask questions that will prompt memories and wait patiently for answers, because their focus is on a few pupils, or even one student, rather than the whole class. They can remind them of past successes and how they gained them, and so help them to transfer skills from one situation to another.

Developing motivation

One of the most important roles of an LSA is to motivate students. They can patiently remind pupils that it is worth doing this because it will help them gain the qualifications to go to college, to pass a driving theory test, to read the menu on their computer game, to read their favourite story on their own – whatever the driving force is for that student. They can also drip-feed encouragement. This can be difficult when the student responds to any praise negatively. This can be overcome by using 'I' statements such as 'I like the way you have…', 'I can read this really well now…', 'I can see you have…'. Another way to do this is to praise specific things that cannot be refuted: 'You have answered three questions correctly. Good start.' Still another is to praise as you pass, so they do not have time to respond negatively.

I have also noticed how LSAs can motivate students by reminding them how well they are doing: 'You have coped really well after being upset at playtime.' It can be helpful to reinforce strategies used successfully: 'You took a few minutes to sit quietly and then came back to class. We must remember that if you are upset again.'

Developing literacy and numeracy

Whenever possible, LSAs will be working on literacy and numeracy skills, whatever the subject being studied. Practising reading, writing, calculating, measuring, and so on can be part of every subject.

Developing oracy skills

LSAs can support the development of oracy. This can be easily done by asking learners to phrase answers in whole sentences or asking them to think of a sentence that includes specific vocabulary. For students who struggle to sequence, an LSA could ask a student to explain what they are learning and jot down relevant words on a whiteboard as they do so. They can then ask the student to order the instructions or information and adjust the order of the words on the whiteboard appropriately. The student could then explain again, using the prompts written by the adult.

Explaining the task as the student works

The adult can help the student by overtly voicing what they are doing. 'That is right, you need to divide the numerator and the denominator by the same number.' This means the student has their action validated and also has another chance to learn the correct vocabulary and remember the process.

Using questioning

Any adult in the classroom can use questioning to support learning. Many of the questions in Chapter 10 are helpful to draw out learning and understanding in those who are struggling with a particular topic.

Support for developing memory skills

A common feature for many pupils with additional needs is that they have memory difficulties. This means they struggle to move information from short-term or working memory (which lasts 20–30 seconds) to long-term memory. Adults can help by chunking the information (for example, how we break down a long telephone number into three- or four-digit groups), repeating the information, suggesting or creating a mnemonic – especially a visual or funny one – or linking it to other information already known. Again, they can prompt students to develop independence by asking them what they could do to help themselves remember this, or by reminding them of a previously successful strategy.

Preventing mistakes embedding

One extremely important task for all adults in the classroom is to prevent students from practising and reinforcing mistakes. This means that they need to be vigilant, gently unpick misunderstandings, and then create some way of going over the correct method that will help ensure it sticks.

Placing the learning in the bigger picture

It always helps students to link the task of the moment to a bigger picture. This might be in the form of a reason for learning ('It will help you do this so you can achieve that') or how this subject links to others ('In history we learned about Norman castles – this lesson about settlement in geography will help us understand how they decided where to build them').

Swapping roles

Sometimes it is helpful for the LSA to circulate the room while the teacher works with an individual or small group who are experiencing difficulties.

Working with colleagues who are supporting learning outside the classroom

Many LSAs will work with students doing one-to-one or group sessions outside your classroom. These sessions are generally focused on literacy, numeracy, or social skills. However, if you are lucky, they can link in and support the work you are doing in the classroom more specifically.

Pre-teaching

This means tackling new vocabulary or concepts before they come up in the whole-class lesson. Pre-learning builds confidence and improves the student's learning experience (see Chapter 3). Pre-teaching is a type of joint working between teachers and LSAs that depends heavily on communication: teachers need to pass on long-term lesson plans together with vocabulary lists. It is not always straightforward to do this if the student has many subject teachers and possibly more than one LSA working with them – it has been the one of the most difficult things I have ever tried to organise as the person coordinating learning support in a school. I am also guilty of being one of the class teachers who has let it fall off the end of my to-do list at times. However, when this works well, it is incredibly effective.

One way to do this is to give allocated time to support staff to look at planning, topics and textbooks, and then consider how the subject matter can be incorporated into the sessions with the students.

Another option, which many schools employ, is to allocate support staff to specific classes or subject areas so that, over time, they can develop familiarity with the subjects covered and can prepare for tricky topics or support children through processes they are likely to find difficult to organise.

Post teaching

Reviewing what has been learned is always helpful as most pupils who need extra support need time to go over topics a number of times. This is sometimes called overlearning (see Chapter 3). Support staff can use the students' own glossaries. Sometimes the students just need to repeat the activity – just tweaked slightly so it is not exactly the same.

Transferring skills back to the whole-class lesson

It is also helpful to transfer vocabulary and skills learned in the group or one-to-one session to the classroom context. If you know what has been the focus for learning then it can be consciously included in a lesson. The communication, in this case from the support staff to the teacher, is again the key to this.

One way to communicate what has been done is for those working with the student to email their records of what they have done in the session to the class teacher (as shown in the example in table 5). This need not be an onerous task. These sessions often have a routine and content that can be planned for several sessions at a time. Once the learning target is set and the activities to support it have been decided upon, each session's record simply needs a specific comment as to what has been achieved, as shown in the example.

How to

Using other people to support differentiation

- Reading practice with adult and student volunteers

- Precision-teaching support

- Mentoring focused on motivation and self-esteem

- Giving support to parents and carers helping with differentiation

- Working with colleagues to support differentiation in the classroom:

  - pen portraits

  - checking understanding

  - breaking down the task

  - developing self-help skills

  - developing motivation

  - developing literacy and numeracy

  - developing oracy skills

  - explaining the task as the student works

  - using questioning

  - supporting memory skills

  - preventing mistakes being embedded

  - placing learning in the big picture

- Working with colleagues outside the classroom:

  - pre-teaching

  - post teaching

  - transferring skills back to the classroom.

Chapter 7

Routines

Many people function more productively when they have a routine they are comfortable to follow. This is especially true for those who find change difficult, such as many people on the autism spectrum. Visual timetables and strategies to prepare for change can provide reassurance and release the student to concentrate on the learning task.

For those who struggle to settle to task and have difficulties concentrating, a routine can bypass unnecessary distractions.

Teachers can develop routines to help organise themselves, which will also benefit the pupils. They will help those who are slow to process information, for example. If the students already know how the beginning of lessons or activities will work because they always follow the same pattern, they can focus on what is to be learned rather than on how the first activity will happen.

For teachers, having a set routine reduces planning and preparation and encourages a calm atmosphere in the classroom. They can develop routines to help with starters, energisers and plenaries that will significantly reduce their planning load. Teachers who develop the habit of including differentiation strategies and ensuring that interventions happen will ensure that their pupils have the maximum chance of succeeding.

Routines to help support pupils

Visual timetables

Pupils who become anxious about change, or confused about how the plan of the day works, benefit from their routine visually presented. This strategy seems to be particularly helpful for those on the autism spectrum, but is also helpful for those who have memory or language difficulties.

The reason visual timetables are so helpful is that anxiety about what is going to happen in the future can overwhelm the pupil's ability to concentrate on the current activity. The pupil can refer back to the visual timetable as many times as they wish to reassure themselves about what will happen for the rest of the day. This idea can, of course, be expanded for a week where the routine may change – perhaps at the end of term when there are celebrations or special assemblies.

Visual timetables can vary from large pieces of card with pictures of the activities, which can be pegged on a string or stuck to a wall where the child regularly works (figure 16), to a very small card for teenagers who want more discreet support.

There are many visual timetables available on the Internet[27] and once they have been printed out and prepared, they are very quick and easy to use.

| Reading | Numeracy | Break | Music | English | Lunch |

Figure 16: Example of a visual timetable

Many pupils appreciate a breakdown of what will happen within a lesson as well – especially if it does not follow a routine. This can be noted on the whiteboard.

Starter: Use Shakespeare's vocabulary in a sentence.

Reading: Opening of Act 2 – add to summary of plot.

Planning together: Analysis of Romeo's character.

---

[27] For example, on www.sparklebox.co.uk.

Warning of change

Sometimes, simply explaining or visually representing what is going to happen may not be enough to allay the anxieties of new and different events. One way to quite quickly reassure those who are feeling worried is to literally walk through the events. For example, before a sports day, an adult could take a group of pupils to where they will wait for their turn to run a race, where they would go to hand in their result, and sit while spectating. Or pupils could look at where they change into their costumes and wait to go on stage for a class play. 'Walking-talking examinations' give the students an opportunity to sit in the exact place they will sit, in the same conditions they would have, to take an important paper. The exam paper itself should also be set out exactly as it would be on the day, if at all possible, so that any problems with finding their way around the questions and tasks can be sorted out. An example of the sort of problem that can be resolved like this is pupils forgetting to number questions so that they lose the marks for all but the first question – easily sorted out once they realise the importance of doing this.

Pupils who present as having behavioural difficulties sometimes need a walk around the outdoor space discussing what would and would not be acceptable and safe behaviour in each area. A short walk like this does not mean they will not forget or choose to disobey rules at times, but it does make the situation clearer and generally reduces the number of infringements.

Offer students who struggle with moving to new activities a simple prompt five minutes before the allocated time to help them prepare and cope. Occasionally, students need a ten-minute and then five-minute reminder in order to switch activity smoothly. This can be supported by using sand timers or pointing to the clock and explaining 'when the big hand...' (A surprising number of teenagers as well as young children find using analogue clocks quite tricky. If you are doing a timed activity such as an examination and they are required to keep time using an analogue clock, it can help to change the time on the clock so the exam will finish on the 'o'clock' rather than, for example, 2:18pm.)

Visual organisers

Those with ADHD and allied difficulties often have enormous difficulties in organising themselves. They might put a lot of effort into doing homework and then simply forget to hand it in. Or they will forget to bring games kit or their library book. This can mean that their whole time at school is punctuated by frustrated adults nagging them. Although it is possible to manage this if parents and staff pack their bags and remember everything for them, it is more helpful to gradually move students on to take responsibility for themselves. This could be done by having a list of what they need to take home each day next to their desk. They need another list in their bedroom (and probably on the fridge and by the front door as well) of what they need to check for each day (figure 17). The school can help parents by offering a version of the list to take home or posted on their website so that parents can then adapt it. Eventually, the child can then create their own. Older students could have a version on their phones if they are allowed these in school.

> Check your bag before you go to bed at night. You should have:
>
> Every day: Pencil case with pen, pencil, ruler
>   Reading book
>   Spare spectacles
>
> Monday: Maths homework, spelling book
>
> Tuesday: English homework
>
> Wednesday: PE kit (trainers, T shirt, shorts)
>
> Thursday: Maths homework
>
> Friday: English homework

Figure 17: Example organiser for display at home

At school there should be a routine so that younger pupils unpack their bag at the beginning of the day, hand in homework, and put their reading book, PE kit and snacks in the appropriate place. Older students, who move between rooms for each lesson, need to be helped to organise their bag so that homework sheets are kept neatly in a folder, and so on. Otherwise their bags can become a muddle of scruffy and torn bits of paper.

Routines to help distractible students complete homework successfully

Students with concentration difficulties often fail to complete homework successfully at the very first hurdle. They simply do not know what to do. This can be overcome by ensuring parents have access to the school website and posting homework timetables and assignments on there. As well as this, it is important to develop the expectation of independence. So it is still helpful to ask the student to record the homework and make sure it is checked for accuracy, legibility and understanding by an adult.

Some teachers set up study buddies for such students so they have a 'go-to' friend if there are any questions. The identified supporter needs to understand that they are only there to pass on information and a brief explanation; they are not responsible to help complete the homework or hand it in.

Pupils who struggle in this way should sometimes be praised for simply having a go and getting work handed in. Further praise for effort and accuracy can then be offered on top of this.

Routines for teachers

Equipment and moving round the classroom

Effective routines help students of all abilities and with a whole variety of needs to access learning. Those with poor concentration and chaotic organisation will be worrying how they should hand in their book, or panicking about what to do with their homework, rather than learning. It means that everyone feels secure in what they are meant to do. Doug Lemov in his book *Teach Like a Champion* points out that thinking through these routines and then practising them will save hours of teaching time over a year. [28] The routines will be different for different age groups and subjects, but here are some ideas that many have found effective:

- Exercise books are handed in open at the page to be marked.

- Work is handed in to three boxes or buckets, which are coloured green, red and orange. The students choose the colour they feel reflects their understanding or level of work, with green being positive and red indicating their concern.

- If the pupils are seated in rows, books are passed out from, and returned to, the front of each row.

---

[28]**D. Lemov** (2010). *Teach Like a Champion*. San Francisco: John Wiley and Sons.

- Equipment such as pen, pencil and ruler are placed ready on the desk at the beginning of each session.

- Equipment such as pencils and rubbers are kept in a central station on larger tables and only taken when the task is to be started.

- The teacher gets the attention of a busy group by raising their hand and waiting for everyone else to then notice and raise their hand and look quietly.

- The teacher gets the group to be quiet by using a bell, rain chimes, etc.

- For younger children, the teacher gets the group to be quiet by using a nursery rhyme that everyone joins in with actions that ends up with hands in laps.

- For younger children, use a song or the same piece of music every day when it is time to tidy up.

- Ask students to repeat specific instructions in chorus.

- Use colour-coded files or books for different groups or activities to support organisation.

- Label all resources that pupils are expected to collect independently – if you can also label the resources in the student's first language too that is both welcoming and helpful.

- Have a system for the order in which pupils enter or leave the room.

- Be at the door to welcome pupils into your room using names and personal comments whenever possible ('I saw your team did well yesterday, John').

- A homework 'basket' for work to be placed in on the way into class.

Using monitors

Another way for the teacher to help the pupils and help themselves is to give students responsibilities within the class. If you always end up collecting up the books or tidying away pencils strewn across the floor you are both wasting your precious time and teaching students that you are willing to let them create mess for you to clear up. You can allocate monitors to give out or collect in materials, check that all scissors have been returned, and so on. Younger children tend to vie for these jobs. They are excellent opportunities for those with ADHD and similar difficulties to move round the room to a good purpose. Students with low self-esteem also benefit from the opportunity to have a role of responsibility.

Starters

How you start your teaching sessions can build differentiation in without any extra effort. Starters can offer a time for those who struggle with change, or have difficulty moving from focusing on one topic to another, to do this gently and without stress. They can build in challenging activities for those that need them and, if the routine is practised, this can happen without lengthy verbal explanations.

Teachers of younger children often have excellent routines for starting the day. For example, this might involve looking at the date, chanting the days of the week or months of the year, and asking what the day was yesterday or the month after this one. Teachers might also talk about the weather, discussing vocabulary and constructing sentences to describe this. Activities linking to numerals in the date and tens and units (perhaps with visual prompts such as bundles of ten pipe cleaners) can also be included. These types of whole-class activities that are done each day give reassurance to those who struggle with the move from being with a parent or carer to being part of a group. They also give the adult an opportunity to assess the mood of any children who might need the next task adapting or would benefit from individual encouragement or instruction.

Slightly older pupils might be asked to sit in their places and start a numeracy task or read their book while the adult deals with queries and individual issues for a few moments. If students need to move from lesson to lesson, the teacher will need activities that are designed to engage pupils in positive learning activities for the first minutes of a lesson while the register is taken or one or two latecomers arrive. The activities should be calm and quiet to be helpful for those who are anxious or unsettled. They can be based on previous learning or introduce a new topic. It is good to have a pattern to these so that students can settle to task without needing explanations and demonstrations.

Here are some suggestions for starters that settle a class down and do not need explanations after the first time they are used. They can be done in the back of exercise books or on mini whiteboards. They can easily be differentiated, either by asking students to come up with more or fewer questions or suggestions, or by setting two or three activities that gradually get harder.

- Create a calculation for a set answer written on the board.
- Write down three nouns, adjectives or verbs linked to the topic on the board.
- Write an answer to the question on the board.

- Write definitions for subject vocabulary.

- Think of five questions on the topic, together with the correct answers.

- True/false statements – the students come up with two true statements and two false statements about the topic being studied, which they can then use to test a partner or share with the class. Another way to do this is for the teacher to write a variety of true and false statements on the board and the students quietly work out which is which, ready to feed back to the class.

- Find three words to describe a relevant picture.

- Find two ways an object links to the subject studied last lesson.

- Odd one out – which of three or four statements on the board is the odd one out and why?

- Create a visual version of a subject studied.

All of these suggestions can be prepared in advance. Once you are thinking of these, you can do starters for a whole topic's worth of lessons.

Five-question starters

Another way of doing this that can stretch more-able students is to set five questions or tasks at the beginning of every lesson. The types of question should be in the same order each time and students know that they are required to do questions 1, 2 and 5 or 3, 4 and 5, or whatever fits their capabilities and needs. Topics, vocabulary and spellings can be repeated. Again, these could be prepared for ten or more lessons at a time.

A possible pattern of a five-question starter could be:

1 Literacy question – name a noun, verb and adjective linked to the topic.

2 Spelling task – copy out a tricky word linked to the topic three times.

3 Linking question – how could this topic link to another subject (e.g. geography, mathematics, etc.)?

4 Vocabulary question – write a sentence to explain a subject word.

5 Open question – question with more than one sensible answer.

Here's an example of a five-question starter linked to a topic (development of castles in England with the Norman Conquest):

1 Name a noun, verb and adjective linked to Norman soldiers.

2 Copy out 'medieval' three times.

3 How does the topic of castles link to geography?

4 What does 'motte and bailey' mean?

5 How would England be different if the Normans had lost the Battle of Hastings?

Energisers

Learning does not have to be quiet and formal – it can be energetic and informal. However, it is worth building in expectations as to how the classroom will return to a quiet focus at the end of these activities. These more lively activities are very helpful for those who have short concentration spans, as they break up the learning into manageable sections. Energisers are also helpful for those who are physically restless and find it hard to sit down for long periods. They can be built into a routine, for example, planning an energising activity after a period of silent working. Here are some suggestions – the first one is the only one that requires time to prepare.

Dominoes

This involves a prepared set of dominoes that link together by matching topic information instead of the usual number dots (as in figure 18, where 'ice' links to 'frozen water', and so on). The cards are shared out and the game is played in small groups or as a large-group activity with large cards stuck to the board.

Still image

Everyone has to create a still image (a representation using their body – but completely still) of something linked to the lesson. It is helpful to give an example of something easy to do for those students who are easily embarrassed, and an example of something a little sillier for those who love to get peer attention. For example, still images on the topic of evolution could include a monkey, a human and an amoeba.

Two truths and a lie

Each pupil has to think of two true facts and one piece of false information about the topic, then test a partner on their ideas.

Throw the ball

The teacher asks a question and then throws the ball to a named student who should catch it and then answer the question. It can be passed back to the teacher or on to another student together with a new question.

Flyswatter learning[29]

Groups of students use large pieces of paper and write the answers to questions appropriate to your subject scattered all over them (cheap paper tablecloths are ideal for this). One student in the group is the question master and the rest stand round the edge of the piece of paper, flyswatters at the ready. The question master asks the questions and the students vie to be the first to 'swat' the correct answer. This is hugely popular and great fun and, when I have been teaching, has only once resulted in a visit to the school first aid station.

Demonstrate the vocabulary

A student comes to the front of the classroom and the teacher whispers a chosen word to them. The student can choose to draw the meaning on the board, explain it without actually using the word, or represent it with interpretive dance (a surprisingly popular option in some groups). Whoever is the first to work out the correct word takes the next turn, or students can have a go in turn.

Water	H_2O
2 hydrogen and 1 oxygen	Evaporated water
Steam	Ice
Frozen water	Expands
Freezes	Aquifer
Water trapped underground	Liquid

Figure 18: Example sheet of six domino tiles

---

[29] I originally came across this idea via #poundlandpedagogy.

Plenaries

Plenaries are activities that sum up and help pupils reinforce and demonstrate their learning. How can they be considered part of differentiation? Firstly, they are an opportunity to revisit the learning in a different format – students with learning difficulties seem to benefit from tackling the same topic in a number of ways and short plenary activities are particularly helpful. I have noticed that pupils with general learning delay sometimes seem to suddenly grasp the topic during the plenary. It is as though summing up the topic or explaining it back to someone in a different format helps them, even though I may have already used a number of approaches to the topic during the lesson.

Plenaries are useful for the teacher in that they are a good way of assessing the learning that has taken place (formative assessment), so your teaching for the rest of the lesson or in the future can be more effective. They can happen throughout the lesson as 'mini plenaries' before moving on to the next section, or at the end of a lesson or topic. Suggestions for these include:

- Recall as many key words used in the lesson as possible.

- Link back to a question posed as part of the starter – ask the students to answer it in a sentence, possibly by displaying their answer on a mini whiteboard so the teacher can check on everyone's learning.

- Identify your best sentence or paragraph from the written work completed – what makes it good?

- Ask students to create three questions for you to start the lesson next time.

- How might what you have learned in this lesson link to another subject?

- How might what you have learned in this lesson help you outside of school?

- Ask students to use three or four given numbers in a calculation to find a total number, using the mathematical process you have been practising.

- Ask pupils to think of a relevant word for the topic linked to each letter of the alphabet.

- Shake two or more dice (the large foam ones are excellent) and then ask students to add, multiply, and so on (using mini whiteboards will ensure everyone takes part).

- When students are preparing for external examinations, you could ask them to write a question on the topic in the format of the exam – you could ask the more-able students to create a mark scheme as well.

- Give an answer and ask the students to come up with a question linked to the day's topic.

It would be worth preparing a slide presentation of plenary activities so you have a selection to choose from without any further work.

Building in differentiation strategies as part of routines

As you teach your students, you can build in differentiation as part of their routines. For example, if you expect students to proofread their work, some might be expected to check all the grammatical marks in a piece, including semicolons and speech marks. Others may only be required to check for capital letters and full stops. Some may be required to use detailed dictionaries, while others may be offered a simpler, larger-font version. Once you have determined who is able to do what, you can ask students to write their own proofreading rules in the back of their exercise book.

When you ask students to answer questions in full sentences – perhaps using key vocabulary or the 'word of the week' – you can differentiate by either giving students varying amounts of time to prepare or asking them a few minutes after others so they have a chance to hear some good examples they can copy or incorporate. This is also a way of managing activities where you ask for an answer from each member of the whole class.

Some pupils might routinely use equipment such as blocks, multiplication squares, special rulers, line guides, and so on. They should be kept somewhere clearly labelled where the pupils can access them independently and clear them away.

Anything you do routinely could be noted on one document that is kept together with the seating plan so that supply staff can easily pick up the routine. It is also excellent evidence of differentiation. The sort of useful information to include would be a reminder of which students might need encouraging to wear their spectacles, that a pupil uses a hearing aid, which students you should check have written down the homework tasks, and who has a study buddy to help with practical tasks such as fetching a laptop.

Routines for the teacher to record behaviour

Sometimes teachers need routines to help themselves – especially if they help students. One routine that can help access appropriate support for students is to build up a diary of concerns. In order to do this in the incredibly busy environment of a classroom, all the adults involved should think of all the concerns for a specific pupil and agree on the ones to focus on and then create a chart. In the following example (table 6), I have included some behaviours written in full, but for the real chart I would indicate these by the initials in brackets, so that any pupil casually glancing at the teacher's desk would not be given information inappropriately. These tally charts are difficult to complete accurately if left to the end of the day, but can be quickly filled in when passing.

Table 6: Example tally chart for recording behaviour

Name:	Date:		
	Morning before break	Morning after break	Afternoon
Lose concentration ('drift off') (LC)			
Ask adult or peer to repeat information or question (RI)			
Delayed response to instruction (follows rest of group rather than moving on own) (DR)			
Demonstrates misunderstanding of information or topic (DM)			

Ensuring support interventions happen

One of the hardest things to do in enabling pupils with special needs to make good progress is to carry out regular interventions that work on specific skills. Working like this daily for a short time is far more effective than longer, but infrequent interventions. However, it takes a will of iron to do this, as distractions so easily arise. If you have another adult supporting in the classroom, one solution is to make carrying out those interventions (with individuals or groups) their absolute priority. If you are on your own in the classroom, set your timetable to carry out the interventions as early as possible each day, so that if other things come up you can still fit them in. If you possibly can, note when you have done interventions – at minimum by ticking a date, even better with brief, but very specific, notes of what you have done. This is invaluable information for assessing what has helped the pupil or what more needs to be put in place.

Waiting for responses from students

When you come across a pupil (or colleague) who seems to take a long time to answer you, count how many seconds they need to process the question. This can vary from person to person, but people with dyslexia or dyspraxia seem to need an average of nine seconds. Once you register how long that particular person needs, you can build it into your interactions.

How to

Routines

Develop routines to help pupils learn by reducing anxiety, confusion and disorganisation:

- Visual timetables
- Warnings of change
- Visual organisers
- Helping distractible pupils complete homework.

Develop routines to improve teaching; pupils accessing learning better and saving you time:

- General classroom organisation
- Starters
- Energisers
- Plenaries
- Differentiation strategies
- Routines to help record behaviour
- Making sure interventions happen regularly
- Leaving a response time.

Chapter 8

Differentiation through managing behaviour

Teaching everyone includes those who have behavioural difficulties. Some schools separate out behavioural and learning needs, but people are much more complex than that. Barriers to learning frequently lead to low self-esteem and, possibly, behaviours designed to avoid problematic situations. Behavioural issues mean students miss chunks of learning, either because they are literally not in the classroom or because they are mentally absent because of their mood.

This chapter offers some suggestions to help teachers enable students to achieve better by encouraging more positive behaviour. This then means that other students also generally achieve more because the pupils who are having difficulties are not distracting them, and the teacher has more time to focus on developing learning rather than managing behaviour.

Some of the following suggestions may seem obvious, but they are all habits or strategies I have had to remind myself of at times when analysing why a class or pupil is disruptive.

Class or group strategies

Helping students to feel liked

This is extremely important. Disruptive students frequently say that a specific teacher does not like them. That very same teacher may say they really like the student even though they cause significant problems within the classroom. Whether the teacher actually likes the pupil or not, the student needs to feel liked. Once they do, they are much more likely to cope with minor issues and stick at a learning task. If they feel disliked, they are likely to have a 'who cares' attitude and invest less in their own learning and take little responsibility for others' needs.

How can teachers help students to feel liked?

One suggestion is to meet them at the door and greet them cheerfully by name and tell them you are glad to see them. If you can add in a personal comment to show you know them individually, that is even better. Positive comments on their performance in a school event, or a quick chat about films they like or teams they support are always appreciated.

Another strategy is to catch the students being good. For some this means making a positive remark as they enter the room, otherwise you could be too late. These remarks could be on some work you have marked or positive behaviour you have noticed, such as being willing to wait patiently for a few moments while you offer someone else help. Encouragement is the focus rather than praise.

The following comments are phrased so that they are about the teacher's perception, so that the student is not able to automatically deny any vestige of a positive attitude or hard work, as some students need to do:

- 'I like the way you waited patiently.'
- 'It looks to me like you really worked hard on your presentation.'
- 'I like the way you always have a cheerful smile when you come in.'
- 'It seemed to me you really stuck at doing this when it was hard for you.'
- 'Andy had an idea about this – I thought it was very helpful.'

What makes students feel disliked?

Sarcasm is often misunderstood. Avoid it. Criticising a student's work in front of others is generally counterproductive. Referring back to previous misdemeanours can lead to students feeling that they can never succeed.

Learn names and use them

This is very difficult for some people (including me). I teach a large number of classes, sometimes only once a fortnight. One way to overcome this difficulty is by downloading school photos of students and keeping them with the class seating plan so you can have a quick look before the lesson. You can also mark books with the photos in front of you, so you can associate the name with the face and work. Also, when meeting a new class, ask how students like to be known, for example, Liz rather than Elizabeth.

Be present

Much of the behaviour that affects the quality of learning happens outside the classroom. Pupils arrive having had an argument in the playground or corridor and, understandably, have difficulty letting go of it to focus on the task. If you are outside your room when they are about to come in, or wander down to the cloakroom to chat and walk back with them, it helps reduce the flashpoints and you can deal with any upsets before they even get to their seats.

Body language and proximity

Teach from the front whenever possible because this will help those with hearing or visual difficulties. Stand where you can easily see and have eye contact with each person.

Be aware that you can inadvertently cause difficulty by how you use your body. If you need to rebuke someone, try to be on their eye level (by sitting down rather than bending over them). Some people find others' proximity difficult, so, if you need to squeeze behind someone's chair or sit very close to work with them, just murmur a word of explanation as you do so rather than taking them unawares. However, merely moving to stand near to someone who is not behaving appropriately can be all that is needed to reduce it. You have communicated that you have noticed and wish the behaviour to stop, without saying a word.

Also, it is worth remembering that body language varies hugely between cultures. For example, some young people have been taught to lower their eyes in respect to an adult. Those with autistic tendencies may also find eye contact very difficult. Loudly telling them to look at you when you are talking to them is not helpful.

Remember the other students

While managing the more difficult students, it is easy to forget those who routinely behave, work hard, and are helpful. They often get justifiably frustrated by the 'naughty' pupils being praised for what they do all the time. Try to pick up on a couple of pupils every lesson and comment on how helpful they have been or their positive attitude. Also make sure that any rewards such as stickers or house points are awarded absolutely fairly.

Praise and encourage positive behaviour

Specifically praising and encouraging the behaviour you would like is very powerful. If you have a brilliant lesson with everyone focused and contributing beautifully, you may go to the staffroom for your break glowing inwardly, but if you end the lesson with a couple of compliments about specific behaviours you would love to see in every lesson it means it is more likely to be repeated:

- 'I was really pleased to see how everyone politely listened to others' answers.'

- 'Good to see how people who found the task difficult looked at the examples from last lesson without needing a reminder.'

- 'Well done for continuing with the task when the lesson was interrupted by a visitor.'

When working with individuals who have great difficulty in keeping to behavioural requirements, pick up on tiny improvements and remind them you are aware of the effort they are putting in and are alongside them noticing it.

Strategies to enable students to work well in groups

Many pupils find working in groups difficult. They may struggle to listen to, let alone accept, others' ideas. Some have difficulty summoning up the confidence to put their views forward. Still others will find it hard to stay focused on the task without the accountability provided by the teacher's supervision. Ideally, we would like pupils to be able to learn to work together productively, but this can be a long process. So, what can be done to make group work more effective and enable all pupils to learn?

Take care with group formation

First, give advance warning of the activity and offer those who will be anxious about this an opportunity to discuss it with you. Then allocate groups – it is very demanding for some pupils to do this for themselves and the activity then begins with an anxious time of being unsure of who they will be working with and worry about how to resolve it. If this type of activity is going to be a regular feature of your teaching, keep the groups the same from one task to the next to provide familiarity and reassurance. Provide a list of specific roles and responsibilities and ask the students to decide who will take them. Some groups may need guidance. You could either set them up with a role description or ask them to write one as part of the task. The group could use a chairperson, timekeeper, IT specialist, display artist, and so on.

Break down the task and the working time

If pupils working individually need a task broken down, this will be even more necessary for groups. They can then allocate parts of the task more easily and tick off what has been completed. If you wanted to, you could set the task up so that everyone has to change task or role at a certain point in the process. You could even randomise this by asking each person to take a card from a shuffled pack and allocate each number to a role.

Also break the working time down so that each group has to report back at set intervals as to what they have done already and what will happen in the next short session.

Ration resources

Offer each group a limited amount of resources. This stops them abandoning a half-completed presentation and starting again with the result that it is nowhere near finished. It also means that the most powerful or quick-thinking characters do not grab the best resources. (It might be helpful to limit the quantity of printing or time online researching. This ensures that anyone using IT has to engage more with the group to decide how to spend the time or printing credit.)

Have rules and incentives

It can help to ask the groups to follow the same rules that you have in class generally during discussions for talking one at a time. The chairperson could take contributions only from people who have raised their hands, or an object could be passed around and students only allowed to talk when they are holding the object.

The teacher can announce that they are observing the groups and will be awarding points in the school's merit system to students who are joining in activities or politely listening to others.

Help students who find working in groups difficult

For students who find noisy and apparently disorganised classrooms difficult, try to place their group in the quietest corner or in the corridor.

These pupils could also have a time-out card for five minutes' calm in a specified place.

Some students become very distressed if they feel that others have broken group rules, even if they are working on the task and being kind to others. It would help if an adult could remind the whole group of the rules and ask students to either use a scripted sentence (e.g. 'one of our rules has been broken. I find it helpful if we all follow the rules'), perhaps provided on a card, or refer to an adult if there are any problems with rules being broken – rather than leave the student to struggle to resolve the situation or decide to withdraw. These pupils generally work better in smaller groups.

Share your behavioural expectations with the pupils

Explaining the rules and expectations means everyone is clear as to what is required. If you can embellish this explanation with visual prompts and humour so it is not a dry and joyless recitation, but an enjoyable and hopefully memorable interlude, all the better. I sometimes ask pupils to act out breaking the rules (they adore doing this) and then ask the rest of the class why this particular behaviour is unhelpful. If you do this, you need to end with some positive statement of expected behaviour so it hopefully remains in their memory.

If behaviour has generally deteriorated, go back to this with the class. Make it clear what excellent, good, and poor behaviour looks like so this becomes an acknowledged and understood vocabulary for everyone.

Model the behaviour you require from pupils

Children and teenagers quickly notice if an adult behaves hypocritically. When you are managing a class full of students with a variety of learning and behavioural needs, you cannot afford to lose your teaching credibility in this way. So although you are in charge of the classroom and can reasonably expect that your instructions are followed, you also need to be liberal with your pleases and thank yous, maintain calm in the face of irritating behaviours, walk away from arguments, and be willing to apologise if you make a mistake or snap at someone.

Strategies for individual pupils

Use a solution-focused approach with individual students

We can helpfully take something from the solution-focused brief therapy (SFBT) approach developed by Steve de Shazer and Insoo Kim Berg. The idea is to look to what life would look like if the problem was solved – rather than investigate the problems – and use this to enable clients to resolve their difficulties. I am not advocating that teachers should act as therapists, and the following guidance is not SFBT – rather, it is a technique that grew out of learning about SFBT to work with students that seem 'stuck' in a cycle of poor behaviour.

When talking with an individual student, ask what life would look like if the problem had been solved. This might take a little while to discuss in detail. Then ask where, on a scale of 1–10 (one being the worst it has ever been and ten absolutely fine) they think the situation is. Then ask what one thing they could do to move it to the next number. Although you are trying to help the student to take responsibility for their own behaviour, you could also sometimes ask if there is something small that you could do to help them move on. In doing this, you are signalling that they are not alone and you are working together to change the situation. Sometimes it helps to write this down and make a little contract you both sign, and agree when to review it.

Allow pupils to get out of a situation with dignity

You are more likely to get compliance from a student if they are not made to look foolish or weak in front of others. Here are some ways to enable a pupil to keep their dignity and do as you ask.

Deal with the primary behaviour and ignore the secondary behaviour

If you speak to someone and ask them to change their behaviour in a specific way, they may try to have the last word or drop some litter, or mutter something uncomplimentary about you as they do it. Having selective hearing or vision at this point and ignoring the secondary behaviour is helpful – they have done what you asked. If you wish you could mildly comment on it at a later date when good relations have been restored. At this point you may well get a sheepish grin and an apology.

Offer two actions, both of which are acceptable to you

Include a thank you when doing this, as this is both polite and shows supreme confidence that your instruction will be followed: 'You could work on the table at the side or move to the spare table at the front. You choose. Thanks.'

Give your instruction and walk away

Go back after a few minutes to check your instruction has been complied with. We all sometimes need a moment or two to sort ourselves out and do the right thing.

Sometimes feign responsibility for a tricky situation

You could apologise for not explaining a clearly reasonable expectation and ask them to comply. I have used this in dangerous situations, for example, with a teenager who had climbed on a roof and seemed to be, from her expression, longing for a confrontation. I called out, 'I am so sorry – I forgot to tell you that you are not allowed to go on the roof. I am really sorry to have put you in a difficult situation. Could you help us out and come down? Thanks.' To my astonishment, she climbed off the steeply sloping roof and came back inside.

Another way to use this is if a student has not acted on either of your options, is to go back after a few minutes with a bit of paper and say, 'I am sorry, I can't have explained things clearly – shall I write it down for you?'

This is not a long-term behaviour management plan but it might save you from a huge confrontation or dangerous situation.

Rebuke privately

If you do have to rebuke someone, try to keep it private. If you are in a large, crowded room and there is nowhere this can happen, move to the side of the person and speak in a very quiet voice (less easy to overhear than a whisper) and when you have finished look at the person, smile briefly and say thanks. (This confuses those who are trying to listen in and again shows confidence that your expectations will be followed.)

Disapprove of the behaviour, not the person

When rebuking a student, ensure your body language and words show that you care about the student but will not accept the specific behaviour. Try to have 'open' body language – with your arms low down, rather than pointing your finger. Sit down alongside them rather than looming over. If you have to stand, try to be sideways on, rather than facing them, if you are a large adult and they are a small child.

It often helps to say something like, 'You know I like you', before launching into an explanation of what went wrong. I often try to finish on a similar note.

Ask for their help

If you have a particularly difficult relationship with a student, try to find out what their interests are or what they are good at and manufacture a situation where you need their help. You could create a numeracy problem based on football scores and ask a sports fan to suggest likely match results or ask a music aficionado for suggestions for good music for background to a slide presentation (checking the lyrics first, of course).

Dealing with attention-needing behaviours

Much of what is considered low-level disruptive behaviour is linked to pupils needing attention from adults or peers.

Behaviours to gain attention from adults

The key to reducing these behaviours is to make it more worthwhile to work independently. I find the best way to do this is to have a conversation with the student at a quiet point and agree together what rules the student will work to. For example, they may be allowed to call out twice, but if they exceed that they will have a small consequence. If they manage to get through the whole lesson without calling out at all, you will praise them. If they do this three times running, you could send a positive email home.

If pupils seem unware they are calling out and they are behaving as though they are the only person in the room with you, limit them to a reasonable amount of chat by giving them three or five counters. They then 'spend' one every time they ask a question or call out. You can sometimes see students weighing up whether to ask a question and deciding to have a go at the task first and then ask a question if needed.

When students do call out, I often ask them if that behaviour was fair to the rest of the class and point out it is not just impolite, it has stopped someone else having their turn or getting help. A word I use unrelentingly in these encounters is 'respect'. Was that respectful to the others in the class? Was that respectful to me, the teacher? I even ask whether they were giving themselves the respect that they deserve because they have not let themselves learn independently or demonstrate mature behaviour. I have sometimes told someone they have behaved with respect at the end of a lesson because they have not called out, and the whole class has broken into spontaneous applause.

Some young children often need adult attention and want to be near you all the time. The way to manage this is to offer the attention or proximity in a way that is acceptable to you. Could they sit near you for a time when the whole class sits on the carpet? Could the seating plan mean there is an empty seat next to them so any adult can sit next to them when working with pupils at their table?

Behaviours to gain attention from peers

A great deal of behaviour that distracts from learning is to gain attention and approval from peers. There are two key strategies here to reduce the behaviour. The first is to do any rebuke privately. (Following this you will also need to reduce any distraction from the learning of other pupils. This can be achieved by moving a student to another place or giving adult attention.)

The second strategy is to set up situations where the pupil can get peer attention by doing the correct thing before they distract others. You can ask them to come and be the scribe for you on the board, help someone who is having difficulty, or do a small job.

Managing rude behaviour

Rude behaviour towards you is normally not about you but an expression of distress. It can be hard to be objective about this. It is worth having a few phrases to hand so that you can acknowledge the behaviour without exacerbating it and also deal with the rest of the class's response. You can then deal with the rudeness later when everything has calmed down.

- 'You seem upset. Would you like a little time to sit quietly?' (Use 'upset' as many students think it is bad to be angry but acceptable to be upset.)

- 'Would you like to write down or draw what has upset you?'

- 'Show me with your thumb (up or down or sideways) how upset you are.' You can then use this as a non-verbal gauge as to whether the student feels they are calming down.

- 'I can see you are upset. I will give you some quiet work to do and then you can join in with us when you are ready.'

Analysing behaviour

If there are specific behaviours you would like to change, one technique is to analyse it using the ABC method (figure 19). You need to consider the *antecedents* to the behaviour, note down what observable *behaviour* the student exhibited, and then the *consequences*:

- *Antecedents:* What happened in the hour or so before the behaviour and also just prior to the behaviour? Was the student quietly on task or were they restless? Were there interactions between the student and others, and so on?

- *Behaviour:* Describe exactly what happened, with whom and in what order.

- *Consequences:* What happened next? Did the student get anything positive out of the behaviour (missed a lesson they disliked, gained control of a situation, gained peer or adult attention?)

Antecedent
End of numeracy lesson where pupil worked well and seemed cheerful
Teacher reminded class that they are going for swimming lesson after break.
(Last week did not go to first swimming lesson of term as felt sick.)

Behaviour
He kicked a chair over and swept pencil pots and piled-up papers off the
table and then left classroom shouting, 'I hate this school.'

Consequence
Withdrawn from swimming lesson

Analysis
The announcement about swimming seemed to be the trigger.
Action:
 • Check how swimming lessons went last term.
 • Chat to pupil about swimming lessons once he has calmed down.

Outcome
Notes from discussion with student:
 • Student loves swimming but was very worried about going swimming
   wearing his trunks that are much too small for him. He set out to avoid
   swimming lesson.
 • Discussed how he could manage a worrying situation better next time.

Actions:
 • Student asked to tidy up mess he had created and given a boring but
   productive task to do during swimming lesson.
 • Teacher had a quiet word with parent about swimming trunks at the end
   of the day.

Figure 19: An example of an ABC analysis

This is a process to do every now and again to deal with behaviour that does not change when you use your normal methods of praise and encouragement alongside negative consequences for poor behaviour. Once you have done this a few times, it can become part of your way of thinking about behaviour and you begin to recognise the patterns leading up to difficult behaviour and move to change the situation. You might suddenly realise that what you thought was a negative consequence was actually a positive for the student because they gained attention – and for some students, negative attention is much better than no attention at all.

Communicating behavioural expectations to pupils with communication difficulties

We sometimes go to great lengths to explain the academic requirements of a task to a pupil – perhaps creating individualised text or illustrating vocabulary with pictures – but fail to do so for behavioural expectations.

When explaining how to behave, you could explain the rules with pictures and then display them. This not only means pupils have many opportunities to read them, but you can refer to them by pointing, rather than wasting time explaining them verbally yet again.

If you have had a discussion with a group or individual pupil about their attitude or behaviour, jot down notes as you do it and then ask them to read it out (perhaps after you have read it to them). The notes could then be quickly photocopied and distributed to each person. This will create a useful record for you and be something the individual pupils can refer back to and read again. It also communicates that this is very important.

Actually, simply writing something down communicates that it is serious. Just saying to a student (with a very serious expression) 'I am going to write this down – oh dear, I am disappointed this has happened', is sometimes enough of a consequence.

Another helpful point is to always phrase the behaviour required positively ('Walk', not 'Don't run'), because those with receptive language difficulties or slow processing will have broken the rule by the time they have worked out what is required. Also, if they only catch one word, it is likely to be the exact behaviour you wish to stop (running).

Explicitly offer a fresh start after a difficult session

Although teachers might assume the student would make a fresh start after a difficult session, the pupil might not realise that and carry over their anxieties and grudges into the next teaching session. Simply saying, 'Fresh start tomorrow', can be all that is needed.

How to

Differentiation through managing behaviour

Class or group strategies:

- Help children to feel liked.

- Learn names and use them.

- Be present.

- Adapt body language and proximity.

- Remember the 'middle group'.

- Praise and encourage positive behaviour.

- Use strategies to enable students to work well in groups.

- Share your behavioural expectations with pupils.

Strategies for individual pupils:

- Use a solution-focused approach.

- Allow pupils to get out of a situation with dignity.

- Deal with the primary behaviour and ignore the secondary behaviour.

- Rebuke privately.

- Ask for the student's help.

- Deal with attention-needing behaviours:

  − behaviours to gain attention from adults

  − behaviours to gain attention from peers

- Manage rude behaviour towards you.

- Analyse behaviour.

- Communicate expected behavioural expectations to pupils who have communication difficulties.

- Disapprove of the behaviour, not the person.

- Explicitly offer a fresh start.

Chapter 9

Developing effective and motivated learners

I f I had to pick a group of strategies that made the most difference to the children and young people I have taught in all sorts of situations over the years, this would be it. This chapter contains ideas to help pupils become effective and motivated learners. The bonus is they take virtually no preparation.

Some children seem to arrive in school able to concentrate and full of motivation to learn. They are willing to keep going in the face of difficulties. These are the children who only have to be shown how to do something once and who can apply their knowledge to new situations.

Others seem to be passive or even resistant and need constant reminders and encouragement. They seem to have framed their views of themselves in negative tones. This is often understandably true of those who are the lowest achievers in a group. They are often willing to study, but expect to fail.

Some others consider themselves to be good students because they have achieved high grades, yet, perhaps because they have not been sufficiently challenged previously, they have not developed habits of persistent, self-regulated effort.

There is often another group who are constantly anxious about their grades and whether they are good enough. These students can hear encouragement to the whole class as an individual message that they are not good enough, and only see themselves as failing. Helping to reduce anxiety helps remove a blockage that prevents learning.

Building in support strategies, such as helping pupils develop their self-organisation in small steps, providing motivation, teaching how and who to ask for help, using role models, and experiencing consequences means that your teaching and their learning become much more effective.

The reality is that most classes contain pupils with a mixture of needs, and teaching strategies that encourage students to become independent, confident and successful learners will benefit everyone in the classroom. This does not replace learning information and skills. It is an effective approach to learning information and skills and develops young people who learn well for themselves.

Developing learning resilience

Developing resilience is, I think, one of the key indicators of eventual success.[30] This can be developed in a number of ways.

Referring to resilience as a normal requirement for success

As you explain a task to a group, you can add in that it might take a number of attempts to get it right or that you are expecting the first draft to need improving. In this way, you are setting up the expectation that a less-than-perfect first attempt is totally acceptable and can lead to an excellent outcome – and it is normal to have to work at this. As part of this, it can be helpful to ask pupils to identify particular moments when they have achieved something they have had to work towards – perhaps saving up towards a treat or learning to ride a bike. You can then encourage them to transfer that understanding to learning in school.

Praising resilience in front of other pupils and showing you value this characteristic means that it becomes part of the vocabulary and normal discussion in the classroom. If you can build in demonstrating resilience yourself, perhaps training for a sporting event or learning an instrument, then it becomes part of the expectation that this is something that children and adults need to succeed. You could also refer to posters with relevant quotations as an active part of this normalising of resilience.[31]

Using self-reflection activities to encourage resilience

Self-reflection activities can be designed to help students to think about how they have learned, as well as what they have learned. Questions that elicit overt commentary on what steps they took in order to complete a task, and then lead them to consider what the next activity should be, are very useful. However, beware of over using them, in case answers become automatic rather than prompt real consideration of how to become more resilient.

Examples of questions to use in self-reflection activities

 What did you find easy?

What did you find difficult?

Think of one action you can do to help yourself tackle the difficult section next time.

---

[30] www.boingboing.org.uk gives further explanation of what is covered by the term 'resilience'. This website also has some articles on examples of resilience in situations other than school.

[31] For example: Genius is one per cent inspiration and ninety-nine per cent perspiration (Thomas Edison).

2 What skills did you use in this task?

Which skills need improving?

How could you improve those skills?

3 What were you pleased about in the way you tackled this task?

What did you find frustrating about this task?

Who will you ask to give you advice on how to tackle the frustrating parts of the task?

The key is to leave some of the responsibility for improvement to the pupil. The tricky part for the teacher is reminding themselves to prompt the class to look back at their reflections and act on them before they do a similar task in the future.

Learn to expect failure on the path to success

The individual's beliefs about failure are one of the key indicators as to whether they will persevere or give up. If a student believes that they can improve by working at something and that it is worthwhile to do so, then they are likely to respond to failure by having another go. The failure is not seen as the end result. This type of belief can be shaped by the adults in the classroom – including this in the explanations and discussions over weeks, months and years.

Big goals reached in small steps

Many of us want to find the one-step answer that will change everything. The truth is, of course, that we often need to make a lot of small changes in order to achieve our goal. There is no one step that will enable a pupil to improve their reading – without regular practice they will not improve. The small steps of learning to decode simple and then more complex words while learning to recognise the words that do not conform to spelling rules cannot be skipped over. The process of working out what the next step is and gathering up the willpower to do it is what makes successful learners. The following suggestions should help you enable students to do this.

- Overtly discuss 'the next step' and encourage students to identify this for themselves.

  - 'What needs to happen next to make this writing the best you can make it?'

  - 'How could you make sure you remember how to do this type of calculation?'

- 'What is the next step in creating this?'

- Encourage them to visualise themselves having reached their goal.

    - 'Imagine – when you can read, you could read *The Twits* for yourself. How brilliant that would be.'

- Use encouraging comments that link the current action to the final goal.

    - 'This may well be useful when you write your assessment piece.'

Reframe their views of themselves

This is the approach I generally use for students who see themselves as failures. By reframing, I mean helping young people to see themselves in another way. Very often this means helping them see the positives in what they have accomplished and the characteristics they have shown . These brief discussions happen during ordinary lessons as I move round the classroom.

The key to this approach is to point out something that the student does well that they have not noticed, and help them see themselves positively before moving back to the difficulty they are experiencing.

Example 1

Pupil: I spent an hour and a half yesterday evening trying to do this and I still didn't get it. I'm just stupid.

Teacher: Wow. You must have incredible concentration to work at something you find hard for so long, especially when you do so much to help at home. What was the problem? Shall we look at it now?

Example 2

Pupil: I got a low mark in the exam – I just can't do it.

Teacher: I heard that you turn up to football practice every single week and now you coach the younger ones. Is that right?

Pupil: Um, yes.

Teacher: That must take real commitment.

Pupil: I suppose so.

Teacher: Do you have to keep working on ball skills with the little ones? Every week? What would you say to a new member of the team who found something difficult?

Pupil: Keep practising.

Teacher: So let's look at which part of this exam needs more practice.

This approach works better if you know the pupils and what they do outside school that you can pick up on positively, but can also work for students you barely know. Here are some suggestions of phrases to change someone's self-view:

- I think it takes real courage to keep trying when something feels so hard.

- Lots of people would have given up, but you haven't. Well done.

- I noticed you helped your learning partner without being asked. That's the sort of person lots of employers are looking for.

- When you are able to do this, you will be such a great example for those who are still finding it hard.

Using a 'prop'

Some teachers have used a physical prop such as a pair of comedy spectacles to help a discussion about how other people might view a situation. The pupil could be asked to think about what they would say to someone else in the same situation.

Example

Pupil: I'm rubbish. I'm hopeless at reading.

Teacher: Let's imagine you are the teacher for a moment. Try these spectacles on to help you feel like a teacher. What would you say to you?

Pupil: Um, reading is really important.

Teacher: What might a teacher say to you about your progress this year?

Pupil: They might say, 'You have moved up a level.'

Teacher: Keep going – what happened last week at the end of the lesson?

Pupil: They might say, 'Well done for reading out loud to the class.'

Teacher: So what might a teacher say to a pupil like you?

Pupil: You are doing OK. Keep going.

Teacher: I agree. Well done.

This type of strategy works well with the students who like a bit of humour and drama, but would be difficult to use with those who have difficulty seeing others' viewpoints, such as some on the autism spectrum.

Developing resilience in those resistant to it

Sometimes you come across a pupil who has so far achieved with ease but is now experiencing poor results. It can be difficult for these students to learn to be resilient. (This is one of the reasons why it is so important to stretch pupils so they need to work at something.) When you talk with a student who has unexpectedly struggled or gained a poor result, they often feel they have worked very hard, although the effort actually put in is minimal. Sometimes they blame their result on the teacher because, in their view, it must be someone else's fault. Their perception of a determined effort has been shaped by their experience of easy tasks.

The change in attitude needs to come from within the student. I have found the best people to effect this are the student's peers. You could ask specific students to explain what they did to achieve their result (choosing the ones you know have spent a good amount of time revising or redrafting) as part of a plenary discussion. Another idea is to set up accountability partners within the class: the students plan a programme of work to complete a task or prepare for an assessment and then assign partners to ask them every couple of days how they are progressing with their work and what specifically they have done. What you are trying to achieve is the pupil acknowledging the need for change and then beginning to take responsibility for it.

Once you think the acknowledgement of the need for change has happened, you can then praise for small steps achieved and offer fresh starts when the inevitable backsliding happens.

Reducing anxieties

A student memorably commented to me that anxiety was like a fog inside her brain. She could not think clearly when anxious. Some students are constantly anxious. This may be a result of extremely difficult situations out of school, or their academic abilities and achievements, or concerns about a friendship group, or their relationship with the teacher. Whatever the cause, it is difficult to overcome and has a negative impact on their ability to learn. The charity Anxiety UK[32] point out that over half of all mental health conditions start before the age of 14, and that anxiety and depression are the most common mental health disorders (and that they are frequently co-morbid – that is, they exist alongside another disorder). Many very young children also experience anxiety, although their presenting behaviour may

---

[32] www.anxiety.org.uk.

be withdrawn, aggressive, or reverting to the habits they had when younger. Pupils of all ages may experience physical symptoms such as headaches.

The following ideas are simply ways for a teacher to help a pupil in class – they cannot, and should not, replace expert help outside the class if needed.

Supporting those with anxiety difficulties within a lesson

Anxiety can be exacerbated by worrying about how to explain this to an adult. You can ease a student's concerns by providing them with a discreet sign, so they can let you know they are worried and need to use an agreed strategy to calm down.

Signs that students can use to let you know they are anxious include:

- placing a red card on the desk
- getting out a red piece of equipment, such as a red ruler
- a coded sentence such as, 'I need to go and see Mrs...'
- thumbs down.

Offer a 'time out card'

The time out card can be small (credit-card sized), and therefore discreet. It should name the contact person and specified safe place for the student, so that adults who are not aware of the issue can be sure the student is going somewhere previously agreed. (Example: 'Fred has permission to leave the classroom and sit in the library for ten minutes. Please let Mrs Smith know if he has used this card in your lesson.') Sometimes all that is needed is permission to stand outside the classroom for two or three minutes, or a few minutes in the reading corner, or just sitting quietly with their eyes closed. You should aim to offer the minimum intervention required.

Remind of past successes

'Do you remember when you...?' can be helpful to gently prompt pupils by reminding them of what went well previously and what they did to help themselves.

Look at the worst-case scenario

This works well for those who are not normally anxious but who currently cannot see a reasonable view of reality. It should not be used with those for whom the worst-case scenario is actually awful – for example, a student worrying about a relative with a life-threatening illness. Neither would it be helpful for a pupil who habitually catastrophises situations or a young person with an ASD diagnosis, as it may reinforce their view rather than redress it.

Also, this can only be done with a young person ready to discuss their feelings with you – which normally implies that there is already a relationship of trust – and should be done within the context of the acknowledgement that their anxiety is real and problematic.

I remember sitting with a distraught teenager. I commented that she looked upset and then waited for a few moments. I then said that I found it difficult to work when I was upset. She nodded. I wondered out loud: what might be causing the distress? She gradually explained what was worrying her. She was worried she might not get the top mark in all her exams. I asked her to explain her worst-case scenario (she might only get top marks in seven out of nine subjects) and then left a long pause and then repeated it back to her before musing out loud all her different options for her future with her worst-case scenario. My suggestions gradually became more and more ridiculous and she started to smile. Sometimes stating the worst-case scenario out loud is powerful. In this case it was that she struggled with less than perfection and some gentle humour began to restore some perspective.

A pattern for the conversation could be:

- acknowledgement that the distress is real

- acknowledgement that there is an anxiety

- offering an opportunity to discuss the anxiety

- together, framing the worst-case scenario and looking at what might result from that

- offering some suggestions or discussing together possible courses of action following the worst case scenario.

Ensure that there is a named adult the pupil feels happy to talk to

When asking students about who they feel comfortable with, I explain I will not feel offended if it is not me, especially if I am their class teacher. Once it is established who the named person is, you will need to let them know and also circulate this information to the rest of the staff. Sometimes students will ask several adults if they can talk to them, which can cause confusion and mean they lose a significant amount of learning time if this happens during lessons.

Use a picture book about managing anxiety

For younger pupils, such picture books[33] can be used with the whole group and then become part of the shared vocabulary when talking about what worries and upsets children. This means that younger pupils can explain more easily what their concerns are and also gives a message that they are not on their own – lots of people become anxious and there are people who will help them.

Picture books can be used with older pupils if they are asked to write reviews on how useful the books would be for younger children. This means they do not feel offended by the simple text and pictures but they have the opportunity to absorb the message.

Planning for non-planners

Many pupils become very discouraged because they find organising themselves so difficult. There are two separate issues here:

1 developing a working routine

2 deciding what to study and how to tackle it.

Most booklets, websites and courses for students to help pupils prepare for examinations or assessments seem to assume that the only way to prepare adequately is to plan ahead – creating a diary with the weeks, days and hours mapped out ahead of time. Advice to those who have difficulty completing their homework follows a similar pattern. I have long felt unhappy with this approach, largely because I know that many children and young people I have worked with simply fill in the plan because they have been told to and then shove it away and do not look at it again. If they do not do this, they often fail to keep to plan a couple of days in and then abandon the whole project as impossible.

So, what can be done to aid these pupils? How can we enable them to develop effective working habits? People rarely change and develop effective learning habits overnight, and so developing these from an early age is important.

Most people live to a routine, even if it is only to go home after school, have a snack and play computer games. Having a discussion as to when doing extra learning tasks would work best, and then including parents and carers in the discussion, can be helpful. For small children, the approach may need to be

---

[33]Among the many books written to help children with anxiety difficulties are *What to Do When You Worry Too Much* by Dawn Huebner, *William Wobbly and the Very Bad Day* by Sarah Naish, and *The Lion Inside* by Rachel Bright.

adult led, but from quite a young age (maybe seven or eight years old for most children) they can be gently reminded by adults but should implement it themselves if possible. The routine could be to have a snack, practise spellings and then read to an adult, and then the child has their free time. Or if the family have a consistent evening meal routine, it could be straight after that.

Building in routines at a young age sets an invaluable expectation that effort needs to be put in and the sooner the child takes on that responsibility themselves, the better for them (as well as the harassed parents, carers and teachers). This can be supported at parents' evenings and in homework and reading diaries or homework links on school websites, as long as there is sensitivity for those caring for children with ADHD or coping with chaotic issues in their own lives.

Those with their own phones can use them as a positive tool. Alarms and timers can be set or homework reminders sent to social media sites. Schools that have a homework program as part of their website can use it to communicate what needs doing when. Sometimes these can also be used to track homework.[34]

Most homework consists of specific tasks, but students need to gradually take control of their learning so they can tackle larger tasks independently. Teachers can help by breaking down larger tasks into several smaller and more achievable activities. Asking students to plan this week's work is less overwhelming than planning four or six weeks' worth of revision. Also, asking them to revise a specific topic by completing a practice question, or ten summary cards, or annotating a diagram is usually more productive than just telling students to revise. You can gradually encourage students to do this for themselves by giving them a revision topic and a choice of activities and discussing with them which ones help them learn most.

It helps to build in some accountability, so telling pupils they have a variety of ways to complete a task, but that you expect to see some evidence that they have done the set amount of work, means that those who would otherwise put it off until a later date are more likely to do some studying.

It is helpful to talk with students about what the priority topics to revise are. Many students simply start at the beginning of their exercise book or textbook. You may want to direct them towards the topics you feel they are less confident with. If the students have done any examinations, it can be helpful to ask them to go through the marked paper and write a list of topics they need to revise using the marks to prioritise them, so the answers with the lowest marks suggest the most important topics to revise.

---

[34] An example of such a tool is www.showmyhomework.co.uk.

Build in motivation

It is often clear to us as teachers why we want our pupils to be able to practise a specific skill or learn some knowledge, because we are aware of the big picture of what we are teaching. For those who are receiving this instruction, it is not always so clear why they are doing what may feel like a tedious task. It can be very motivating to explain where it fits in. 'Once you can explain how blood flows round the body, we will have enough understanding to do some experiments on this.' Understanding that once one can read music, an individual can learn to play any song they like is an exciting prospect for musicians.

Explaining the link between what we are learning today and how that will help achieve their goal sometimes needs to be explained throughout the task – it is so easy to forget the big picture. This is very important for those who tend to focus on the detail and not grasp the whole – a particular issue for many with ASD. If there is a visual representation of the big picture, this can be even more powerful. Some teachers do a sort of ongoing diagram on the classroom wall that shows the whole topic: you can then show how the current lesson fits in with it.

How to ask for help and build up a network of support

One of the factors that is a predictor of success in school is a family that will support a child. For pupils whose families struggle to do this, you could think about helping them build up a network of support. This could include older students, external mentors, and adults in school. It helps to have quite a wide network so that if one person moves on, or is unavailable, the student can look to someone else. This can be done informally when discussing who could be helpful, or introducing the student to other adults in school and setting up situations where they can work together, or more formally as part of a pastoral programme.

Schools sometimes have access to an monitored online support network and this can be a useful extra to offer, especially for weekends and holiday times when the adults outside the family they would normally turn to are not available. Some online support is available to individual users,[35] although a

---

[35] For example, www.kooth.com.

teacher recommending such a website should check that it is allowed as part of their school's safeguarding protocols.

Even when they have a good network, some students don't think of asking for help, or find it difficult to ask for help. Suggesting that students ask for help or guidance can be mentioned routinely when talking about homework, revision, or reading practice. If you are teaching a new way to do calculations or read with children, perhaps you could ask if your school could set up a short evening session for parents and carers. These are often very popular and result in the adults having more confidence to support their children.

Find role models

One of the most powerful things I ever did as a teacher was quite by chance. As some 13-year-old pupils were talking about their assessment results and were clearly feeling discouraged, I mentioned a couple of young people, three years older than them, who had recently achieved outstanding results in their examinations: 'They got very similar results to you when they were your age and then decided to work hard and take every scrap of advice teachers gave them – and look how well they did.' The pupils were amazed, and because they knew the teenagers I mentioned, talked to them and heard the same from them. This gave hope and a positive example and actually became a bit of an in-joke in lessons as I cited the older pupils as examples over and over again. Sure enough, the younger pupils did well in their examinations when they eventually sat them.

I started to encourage other pupils to ask older friends who had done well (and critically, worked hard) what they had done to gain their positive results: 'Don't just listen to me, ask them and follow their example.'

This way of thinking can be extended to finding inspiring young people who have overcome adversity. Malala[36] has been an inspiration to many young people, and students often comment that if she could cope, then maybe they could as well.

Experiencing consequences

The old adage, 'Experience is the teacher of all things', means that we have to let children suffer the consequences of their own forgetfulness or lack of work. The student that has to replace lost equipment out of their own allowance learns to take more care of it or manage without it.

[36] www.malala.org/.

In school terms, this means that whatever consequence happens for those who do not do homework needs to happen relentlessly for all students. Those with conditions that increase the likelihood of disorganisation need it even more. The consequences can be small but must happen, no matter what. Otherwise, all you are teaching pupils is that they do not need to put effort into being responsible for their own actions. However, alongside this you can offer opportunities to do homework with an adult around at lunchtime, reminders of deadlines, and so on.

Feeling safe

Lastly, all of these strategies will be of little use if the children in our schools do not feel safe.

It is hard to change attitudes and take risks by tackling difficult tasks. It is vital that people feel safe as they do this. Safe from teasing. Safe to have despondent moments or even very upset moments on the way. Safe knowing that someone bigger and older than you has got your back while you work on your goal. So this means that in classes where the teacher is fair, where individuals are not mocked but are quietly called to account, and where mutual respect is the usual expectation, pupils are likely to work hard at overcoming their difficulties.

Those that have experienced bullying and social isolation may be worried about breaks and lunchtimes for a long time afterwards. It can help to offer opportunities to be in a safe place such as the school library or to let those supervising the break times know there is an issue.

How to

Developing effective and motivated learners

- Develop learning resilience
  - Emphasise resilience as a normal requirement for success
  - Use self-reflection activities
  - Learn to expect failure on the path to success
  - Big goals reached in small steps
  - Students reframe their view of themselves
  - Use a prop for students to see through another's eyes
  - Developing resilience in those resistant to it
- Reducing anxieties
  - Support those who are anxious in lessons
  - Offer a time out card
  - Remind of past successes
  - Look at the worst-case scenario
  - Ensure there is a named adult to talk to
  - Use picture books with young children
- Planning for non-planners
  - Develop a working routine
  - Decide what to study
- Build in motivation by explaining the bigger picture
- Build a network of supporters
- Find role models
- Teach pupils to expect consequences
- The importance of students feeling safe.

Chapter 10

Teaching high achievers and the gifted and talented

Teaching everybody effectively includes those who achieve easily. Not only that, but if we fail to use good strategies to stretch and challenge these pupils, we are actively instilling habits that mean they have little resilience and a poor work ethic. They may have never routinely had to practise something regularly until they can do it, or puzzle over a tricky problem until the pieces fall into place. We may be breeding disaffection and boredom. Good teaching for these pupils deepens and extends their knowledge and understanding.

In this chapter I suggest teaching habits that mean you can adroitly adapt your teaching to enable all pupils in the class, including the more and most able, to develop, broaden, and deepen their knowledge.

Alongside this, good teachers will teach these pupils to develop independent learning skills – the metacognitive skills that will enable them to reflect on their own learning and develop it further. These include the plan–do–review cycle, critical thinking, and considering what is a good question for a particular topic or issue.

Einstein said, 'Imagination is more important than knowledge. Knowledge is limited. Imagination encircles the world.'[37] Playing with ideas, wondering 'what if', and turning the norm upside down leads to scientific discovery, great novels, and engineering breakthroughs. Our pupils need to use their imagination and develop curiosity.

Some of the pupils who have outstanding skills in one part of the curriculum can struggle in others. I have worked with amazing musicians who are dyslexic and students who excel academically and have additional needs such as difficulties with social skills. This is sometimes known as 'dual exceptionality', or '2E'. These students need careful support if they are to thrive.

---

[37] In a 1929 interview with *The Saturday Evening Post*: www.saturdayeveningpost.com.

Many gifted and talented students, including those with dual exceptionality, need to develop fluency in some areas alongside the opportunity to enrich their understanding. I suggest two simple strategies to enable this to happen successfully.

What is good teaching for those who learn quickly and easily?

Students who are achieving the set task quickly and accurately need something different, not more of the same. It is not helpful to give them simply another page of similar calculations or translation tasks. Also, they should not do the same topics in the same detail but simply faster: this will put them out of phase with their peers and cause difficulties in the future.

These students need the tools and tasks to take them deeper into the subject or to stretch out and link to other topics, subjects, current affairs, historical topics, and so on. They need to be familiar with the language of the discipline and have fluency in the skills required. So, for example, a student who is outstanding in English needs to be able to explore complex poetry, understand how the poems fit into the development of literature, and the references to historical events or experiences. They also need to be familiar with metaphors, analogies, different stylistic forms, and be able to analyse the rhyming scheme with ease.

If it is possible to arrange, such pupils need to be able to discuss and puzzle out problems with like-minded peers. It can also instil a healthy competition to realise they are not automatically the best in the group. This is not always easy to set up and might mean linking students with others in different schools.[38]

Teaching to broaden knowledge and understanding

Teaching in this way enables students to grasp the big picture – like a spider's web, linking disparate disciplines and knowledge. Each strand linking different pieces of knowledge strengthens understanding. So reading *To Kill a Mockingbird* gives an understanding of life in the deep South of the USA in the 1930s and a background to the work of Martin Luther King. Watching a documentary on the life cycle of a butterfly gives a better understanding of the interdependence of plants and animals in an ecosystem.

How can this be done routinely? One way is to give open-task homework so that the pupil can choose between a number of relevant tasks, which can include some of those that link understanding (see the suggestions

---

[38]www.potentialplus.uk.org, www.nagc.org, and www.aaegt.net.au all include helpful advice and organise groups and activities for children and young people.

for alternative recording methods in Chapter 2). You could offer guidance to those you feel would benefit from watching a documentary online and possibly writing a review or answering a question on it, or reading an article from a magazine.

If a student is clearly completing homework or class tasks quickly, perhaps they could have a linked activity – a book to read, a research topic or a creative writing project they can turn to when they have completed the set task. If you have easy access to computers and headphones, there are numerous options for material to enrich and broaden the lesson.

Another option is to have a set of worksheets that involve puzzles, reading advanced text, or research questions, so that you always have a suitable task to suggest. Once created, these will be a permanent resource. You could even set the task of creating new tasks as an extension activity.

Figure 20 shows an example of work by a seven-year-old asked to do independent research on ancient Egyptian inventions still used today.

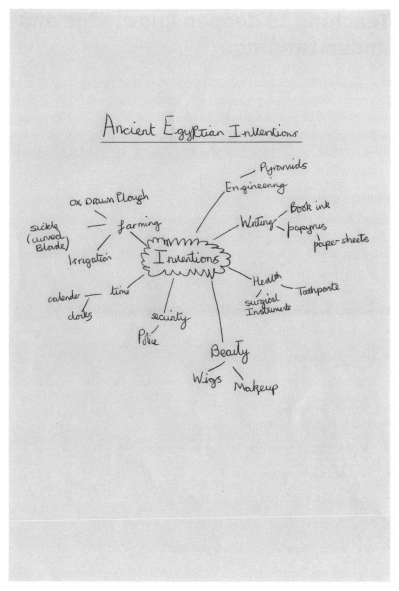

Figure 20: A seven-year-old's investigation of ancient Egyptian inventions still used today, done as an extension activity

Teaching to deepen knowledge and understanding

Our highest-achieving students need to do more than simply acquire more and more knowledge. They need to work out how it links to what they know already, use it to evaluate other new elements, and use it as a launchpad to comprehend more abstract and paradoxical concepts. These higher-order thinking skills are an important way to challenge and stretch pupils and develop critical thinking.

Prepare questions

Higher-order thinking skills can be incorporated into lessons by using questioning. I have found it helpful to collate questions for different purposes and have these available so as to be able to differentiate with the minimum of preparation.

Questions to consider the quality of information given

- What evidence is there?

- How could someone disprove this?

- What sort of evidence is this? (documentary, scientific, theoretical, historical…)

- How reliable is the source?

- Are there multiple sources for this information?

- What assumptions were made?

- Under what conditions does this become invalid?

- What values or belief systems underpin this information?

- Who might disagree with this explanation?

- Are there any principles or theories that underpin this information?

- Is there any evidence of bias or distorted thinking?

Questions to consider the importance of the information given

- Does this change your views in any way? Why?

- If this information had been available to… would it have changed how they worked, or what they explored, or how they created?

Questions to help others understand the concept

- What would the best metaphor or analogy be?
- Is there a similar pattern anywhere else?
- What is the most important part of this information? Why?
- Can you think of another example?

Questions to help apply information

- How would this principle apply if…?
- How does this concept apply to this new problem?

Questions to help look from other perspectives

- What would the argument against this be?
- Who might disagree with this? Why?

Questions to help analyse and synthesise

Questions to help analyse explain constituent parts of the information, while those that synthesise look at information from a range of sources:

- Can you list the different parts?
- What do you need to understand before this theory makes sense?
- What was the most important event or moment?
- Can you categorise the different parts?
- What is the function of this?
- What special features are there?
- What similarities and differences are there?
- What could be combined effectively?
- Using the knowledge from these examples can you create…?
- How would this be different if…?
- What disparities are there in this information?

Questions to clarify thinking

- Why do you think that?
- Can you rephrase that?
- Can you give an example – real or hypothetical?

Questions to consider implications

- If x is true, what happens to y?

- What would the impact of (a) be on (b)?

Questions to challenge the question

- Why did I ask this question?

- Is this an important question?

- Is there a better question to ask?

Use layered questions to help all abilities in the class

SOLO taxonomy[39] is a strategy that supports students to move from understanding one piece of information to several, and then integrate this knowledge into a structure which can then be generalised into a new domain. You can use this principle by using layered questions; building on questions so as to include everyone in discussing a topic ensures differentiation within a whole-class activity.

Start with simple questions and then build up to develop the concept and leave those who need challenging with a particularly tricky quandary while you go back to the other class members and continue the discussion at a simpler level.

An example of layered questions on Pride and Prejudice by Jane Austen

1 Who are the main characters in the novel? (information).

2 Why does Lizzie dislike Mr Darcy? (simple analysis).

3 Why does Lizzie dislike Mr Collins? (simple analysis).

4 Why does Mrs Bennet want her daughters to get married? (inference and deduction linked to historical knowledge).

5 How does Lizzie's view of the purpose of marriage differ from that of her mother? (comparison using inference and deduction).

6 What assumptions about marriage are explored in the novel? (exploring the world view of the era).

---

[39] SOLO taxonomy is a concept developed by John Biggs and Kevin Collis in *Evaluating the Quality of Learning: The SOLO Taxonomy* (1982, New York: Academic Press). Pam Hook has written a very helpful book with Julie Mills called *SOLO Taxonomy: A Guide for Schools* (2011, New Zealand: Essential Resources Educational Publishers) and her website pamhook.com has some excellent free resources.

(7) Would the plot of the novel work as well if the Bennet daughters were able to have a job and earn money? (application of knowledge to a different situation).

(8) What other artistic movements were happening as this novel was published in 1813? (link to movement from classical to romantic era in music and poetry).

An example of a layered question using The Lion, the Witch and the Wardrobe *by C.S. Lewis*

(1) Who are the main characters in the story? (information).

(2) What leads Edmund to betray the other children? (analysis).

(3) The children were wartime evacuees. How does this influence the plot? (analysis linked to historical knowledge).

(4) C.S. Lewis was a Christian. Can you see any Christian themes in the book? (exploring the world view of the author).

Strategies to encourage higher-level thinking skills

It is a helpful and energising strategy to give extra time to the whole group to think of an answer – possibly 30 seconds, or even longer. For those who get to the answer almost instantly, ask them to put it into a complete sentence using two or more examples of subject-specific vocabulary, or come up with five more correct answers, or be ready to demonstrate how they got to their answer on the board.

It is important to be willing to accept half-formed answers – brand new concepts take time to assimilate and some students may be almost thinking out loud. You can affirm the pupil ('I like the way you are thinking') and then ask if anyone can add to the answer, thus showing you think it is of value and it is acceptable to take time to develop thought, but also that there is more to hear and understand.

Pose, pause, pounce, bounce (PPPB)[40] is a questioning technique that combines giving time with developing the answers given:

(1) The question is *posed*, including any context needed.

(2) The teacher *pauses* for thinking time and does not allow any hands up during this time.

---

[40] I first came across this in @teachertoolkit who acknowledges Dylan Wiliam, who credits an unnamed teacher for coining PPPB.

3 The teacher asks student A for an answer immediately (*pounce*).

4 The teacher then asks student B to evaluate the answer given (*bounce*).

The teacher can choose the question and students to stretch students of any level – but the pounce, bounce section ensures engagement from everybody. You have to be ruthless with the no-hands-up policy and any noises or muttered responses, reminding those responsible that they are stopping others learning well.

Another possibility is to ask an able student to prepare a question-and-answer session armed with some starter questions and a couple of textbooks. This would develop leadership skills as well as subject understanding.

Teaching metacognition

Metacognition is the ability to reflect on how one learns and apply this to new situations. This can be an understanding of how much knowledge you have and what you need to find out, as well as an appreciation of how you learn most effectively.

An example of this is the 'plan–do–review' cycle. For many able students, teaching some of the metacognitive strategies simply overtly voices their working practice and enables them to recognise what they do to learn well. For others, teaching a range of strategies to develop questions to investigate, set goals and ways to check their own progress enables them to become independent learners.

The key to doing this well is to know and understand the specific pupils in the class. One exceptionally able person does not necessarily learn just like another. Like any other pupil, their personality and interests will affect the way they learn best. Listening to their ideas and watching how they work and then discussing what seems to work well for them and suggesting how to tweak this is very helpful – just because a pupil is very able does not mean they necessarily understand how they function best or are able to reflect on what works for them.

It is, however, reasonable to sometimes say they need to do a piece of work in a specific way, whether that suits them or not – for example, setting out scientific experiment reports in a specific way means that they can then be easily understood by others. This means they can then cope with the requirements of studying as they move on to different situations.

The ability to transfer skills, knowledge and understanding to other contexts enables students to start any new topic or subject from a strong position.

Building in questions like, 'What do we know already that will help us tackle this?' builds an expectation of using prior learning to access anything new.

A key skill within metacognition is the ability to work out what you don't know and pose the questions that will lead to the discovery of the information or understanding. This skill is useful for all abilities and needs practising. Oddly enough, it can probably be most easily taught at the end of a topic rather than at the beginning or part-way through. Reflecting on what the group has learned by asking what questions would have been the most helpful to ask about gravity, computing volume, or volcanoes gives the prompts for the beginning of the next topic about the type of questions that will provoke interesting thinking. Also, asking students 'Now you know this, if you were trying to discover new information, what would be the next step to think about?', 'Where might you go to work out the next question if the Internet was not available', ' Are there any links to information or skills in other subjects that could help?'

Metacognition can be successfully woven into everyday teaching for the youngest pupils as well as older ones. The process is the same – reflection on how they tackled a task and how to do it better next time; what questions might they need to answer?; what different ways of answering those questions could they think of?; what do they know about the topic already that might be relevant?

So how can this be built into lessons? Ways include:

- a starter activity where students discuss in pairs what they know already and what they think is the most important question to answer

- self-assessment ratings at the beginning and end of activities – a simple gauge of how confident they feel to tackle, say, simplifying equations at the beginning and the end of the task – and then, importantly, what helped them improve (always assuming they have)

- asking students to think about what helped them learn well during the lesson, as a quick plenary activity

- a plenary pulling out different ways to tackle the same problem offered by the class

- using sticky notes for students to write down questions and then brainstorming as a group how these could be answered (not necessarily giving the answer), offering time to try some of the strategies suggested, and then evaluating how useful the strategies are.

As a teacher, you can often help metacognition develop by overtly explaining to individuals how you have observed them learning effectively. An example of this is when I commented to one young man 'You seem to simply take in lots of information and then just wait until your mind clears into a pattern.' He looked a little bemused but later in the lesson said, 'Yes. That's right.' Interestingly, a student who had significant difficulties, sitting nearby, said later that she also worked like this – as she said, she sometimes she just needed to let the knowledge 'settle down'.

Time to think is very important. Getting the right pace of teaching can mean building in time to ponder and consider. Some teachers do this by having times of silence; others use a specific piece of music that signals independent thinking time. Some students are showing their metacognitive skills when they are able to say, 'Can you give me a minute, Miss? I need to sort this out in my head.'

How to integrate imagination and curiosity into lessons

These suggestions should enable students to choose to not simply conform to the set syllabus but to develop their own way of thinking, to explore for themselves whatever fascinates them, or to ponder on what they have observed. Our ability to think differently, divergently, reduces as we mature throughout childhood. Schools often encourage conformity of thinking and behaviour in order to manage the syllabus and the numbers of pupils. Any activities that engage the imagination and encourage curiosity are therefore very valuable.

A teacher that knows their pupils well enough can make individual suggestions that link to personal interests. One student I teach has been studying computer science to a very high level in his own time, supported by the IT teacher. He recently came into a lesson and pulled a textbook out of his pocket and said, 'Miss, what is Cartesian duality? Look, it mentions it here in my IT textbook.' Not only was the student achieving at a high level in his field of interest, he was also, as a result, curious about the philosophy of René Descartes. That discussion, which expanded to the rest of the class, had a positive impact on everyone's learning. The student grasped new connections between different subjects and the class learned a little more about philosophy – all due to a motivated, intelligent student and an IT teacher willing to challenge and encourage. You can never know where encouraging curiosity, a willingness to explore information, can lead. In this case from IT to philosophy.

Suggesting books to read, music to listen to, and films to watch can all engage the student in a different way. One student in the same class came in after watching a documentary I recommended and told me she had changed her views on an ethical topic having thought about what she had learned.

Another way to stimulate learning for all pupils, but perhaps especially for those who are more able, is to include an incongruous, contradictory, uncertain, or complex element into the lesson. This can be done by using a controversial or puzzling statement in the starter and then pick up comments and thoughts at the end of the lesson. Or a wonderful picture or complex diagram could be displayed and left up for students to consider why it is relevant throughout the lesson. I have stuck a well-known chocolate bar on the board and asked students to think in what ways it is similar to or different from the doctrine of the Trinity. Students were engaged and motivated by the bizarre comparison and the more able came up with excellent insights.

You could develop a challenge like the 100DayProject[41] where people are challenged to do something creative every day for 100 days and record their findings either manually in notebooks or through a shared Internet site. Other challenges, like building models of what you are studying (for example, the solar system or volcanoes) can encourage independent research. It is even better if the teacher is able to take part alongside the students, thus demonstrating the excitement of ongoing learning.

Teachers of young children can develop scenarios for pupils to role play. This can enable them to enter into the issues in a deeper way.[42] Creative writing, historical and geographical knowledge, and problem solving can all be used as part of this.

Dual exceptionality

Dual exceptionality means that a student excels in one area but struggles in another. These students often have excellent vocabularies, are creative, offer superb verbal answers, have a sophisticated sense of humour, are able to problem-solve, and are very interested in a specific subject. If they undergo cognitive assessments, their classic profile will have significant peaks and troughs. For example, they may have a very high vocabulary score but a low reading accuracy score.

Dual exceptionality students may be recognised as having a special need but their giftedness sometimes goes unnoticed, especially if it is in a non-curriculum area.

---

[41] the100dayproject.org.

[42] A number of examples of working this out in practice are explained at ramblingsofagiftedteacher.wordpress.com.

I have noticed three common areas of need for these students, which are dyslexia, autism spectrum disorder and social and emotional needs. Of course they could also have a variety of other needs such as ADHD, dyspraxia, and so on.

Dyslexic students may need help with literacy skills so they may need to use dictation packages to record their work (see section 'Consider writing using IT or a scribe' in Chapter 2). Many people with dyslexia also struggle with organisation and short-term memory and benefit from the sort of visual prompts discussed in Chapter 1. They may also need support to break down the complex tasks they wish to do linked to their area of expertise.

Those on the autism spectrum will benefit from the usual strategies used, such as a visual timetable and careful preparation for new situations and change. They may also need guidance on how to expand and develop their higher-level skills and knowledge. As a teacher, you could introduce them to relevant books and websites or groups and clubs who could nurture them.

Students who are more and most able may also have extra social and emotional needs. Although many regard being gifted and talented as a blessing, it can also bring loneliness, frustration and disaffection. Such students might need extra encouragement to work well in groups (see Chapter 3). They might also benefit from a mentor who can encourage them and also call them to account when needed.

Each student has individual needs, and this is especially true for those with dual exceptionality. I think the very best support you can offer is time to talk one-to-one so you can work out together what would help in their area of difficulty alongside strategies to nurture their skills and talents.

Developing fluency

Students who are more and most able need to be able to do the small constituent parts of a task with minimal thought in order to access higher-order thinking and activities. A pupil who cannot recall instantly the answer to 7×7 will struggle to carry out a complex mathematical equation. Their focus will be taken off the job in hand as they work out calculations. Similarly, a music student will need to be able to read music without working out from a diagram what a specific note is.

This can be taken further. The truly exceptional are so at home in the craft underlying their subject that they can break or play with the rules to great effect. For example, Bach's skill in harmonic structure meant he could play with then unknown chords and create glorious music. Shakespeare's knowledge of classical rhetoric meant he could craft phrases that encapsulated the human condition brilliantly. Somewhere in some class are the future great composers, playwrights, software engineers and scientists who need to hone the skills for their subject.

One of the most important aspects of fluency is developing vocabulary so that students have a rich general vocabulary as well as a clear understanding of subject-specific vocabulary. This will mean that they can communicate effectively. Extended and varied reading will supply this and should be encouraged as the norm. Novels that are set in the historical period being studied, biographies of key people, or books that extend factual knowledge will all feed both breadth and depth of knowledge. It is worth creating a list of books relevant to your subject and age group you teach so you have suggestions to hand. These could form part of homework or be available to read in class.

One strategy that really helps is to incorporate the fluency practice into the learner's area of expertise in some way. This builds in motivation. I once helped an otherwise very skilled young farmer to read using the Highway Code (the guide and rulebook for UK road users) so he could tackle his driving theory test. His motivation and willingness to stick at his reading practice tripled instantly.

The other strategy is to do the practice required little and often – always good advice, but in this situation even more important than usual. You could develop a routine where the pupil does ten or twenty minutes of practice before they move on to an activity linked to their own area of expertise.

Ask students what skills they needed to improve in order to tackle specific activities more successfully. If you are learning to play a tricky piano piece with lots of runs, it drives home the need to practise scales until your fingers find the notes quickly and easily without thinking about it. What have the students found difficult – spellings, times tables, referring confidently to the table of chemical elements? Ask them what could they do to increase their fluency so that next time the process is easier.

How to

Teaching high achievers and the gifted and talented

Good teaching for those who learn quickly and easily includes:

- teaching to broaden knowledge and understanding
- teaching to deepen knowledge and understanding.

Key strategies to deepen knowledge and understanding:

- questioning techniques, including layered questions
- ways to develop higher-level thinking skills.

Stimulate learning by:

- teaching metacognitive skills to develop independent learners
- integrating imagination and curiosity into lessons
- being alert to the needs of those with dual exceptionality
- developing fluency in fundamentals (e.g. times tables, spellings) in order to access higher order activities.

Index

Figures and tables

Notes

Notes

Notes